"The smell of bacon. The sight of pancakes growing golden on a griddle. The sound of gentle conversation at a long counter. If there is a place where just about anyone in this fractured country would feel at home, it's in a roadside diner, and if you wanted to dream up the ideal version of such a refuge, it would look and sound and smell a lot like the Phoenicia Diner. From Brunswick stew to biscuits and gravy to 'shrooms on a shingle, this book brings all of those sensory comforts to life on every gleaming page. This book might just save America."

—**JEFF GORDINIER**, author of *Hungry: Eating, Road-Tripping, and Risking It All with the Greatest Chef in the World*

"If there's a sight in the Catskills more soothing, more full of familiar promise than the globe lights shining beacon-bright through Phoenicia Diner's windows, I just don't know it. In the embrace of the Diner's vinyl booths, I have stomped snow from the treads of my boots between bites of Salisbury steak, shared a late-August milkshake with a new love, welcomed in birthdays with pancakes and fat onion rings. The Diner's knack for nudging nostalgia into a modern context is what makes it so special, and it's all over this book: 272 pages of a gorgeous, inclusive, golden-yolked American Dream, where chilaquiles and Brunswick stew and patty melts and meatballs are all welcome and all make perfect sense. The Diner will make short-order cooks out of all of us, and that's a very good thing."

—**JORDANA ROTHMAN**, restaurant editor-at-large, *Food & Wine*

"A really good diner becomes the heart of its community, and Phoenicia Diner is a great one—serving up hearty and delicious food from people who are happy to see you, and a sense of abundance that feels like home, whether you're a local or just passing through."

—**DANNY MEYER**, CEO of Union Square Hospitality Group and founder of Shake Shack

"*The Phoenicia Diner Cookbook*, like the restaurant itself, seamlessly mingles classic expectations with dishes that reflect the way we cook and eat today. Buttermilk pancakes coexist with steak chilaquiles; pimento cheese patty melts with pork belly BLTs; and lemon-meringue pie with autumn harvest muffins. How do they get along between the covers of the same book? Because they all meet the essential criteria of great diner food, delivering big, smile-inducing flavors that make you want to stop and pull over every time you drive by or, in this case, spot it on your bookshelf."

—**ANDREW FRIEDMAN**, author of *Chefs, Drugs, and Rock & Roll* and host of *Andrew Talks to Chefs*

"The Phoenicia Diner has been a beacon for me and my band of road warriors looking for good food. It is everything you want in a modern/vintage diner that is very, very hard to find these days—honest cooking with good local ingredients. A perfect dream sequence of the American road food dream."

—**ANDREW CARMELLINI**, owner and chef, Locanda Verde and The Dutch

"When you eat at the Phoenicia Diner, you can feel the heartbeat of the Catskills, fully surrounded by mountains with a menu full of soulful diner classics. The first time I visited was the middle of winter—a quiet February afternoon, snow falling outside, hot coffee and pancakes inside—nowhere I would have rather been."

—**ELISE KORNACK**, chef, Take Root

"The first time my wife and I rolled into the Phoenicia Diner, we knew they were doing something special—from the energy in the space, the hospitality offered the second we walked in, and, ultimately, the delicious nostalgic food."

—**MICHAEL CHERNOW**, restaurateur, Seamore's, WellWell, and The Meatball Shop

THE PHOENICIA DINER COOKBOOK

THE
PHOENICIA
DINER
Cookbook

*Dishes and Dispatches from
the Catskill Mountains*

**MIKE CIOFFI,
CHRIS BRADLEY, AND
SARA B. FRANKLIN**

PHOTOGRAPHS BY JOHNNY AUTRY

**CLARKSON
POTTER/
PUBLISHERS**
NEW YORK

To Chris and Chrystal Raptis, who entrusted this precious piece of Catskills history to me.

To my mom, Marie, for instilling in me that sharing food around a table is the simplest but most powerful expression of love of family and friends—a gift I will forever carry in my heart.

—Mike

Contents

HEARTY MAINS AND SIDES

PIES, PUDDINGS, AND SWEETS

BEVERAGES

INTRODUCTION

The directions are simple: take Exit 19 off the New York Thruway in Kingston, make a right turn onto Route 28, and head west.

A simple sign on the right reads: "Catskill Park," a rough-hewn outline of the region etched into the wood. To the right, a dilapidated steakhouse sits on the edge of a rock face; to the left, a low-slung motel. Pass "The Dollhouse," a once rickety building of peaks and eaves, now renovated. Habitat for Humanity's ReStore parking lot is full to capacity, as always—people dropping off entire estates' worth of furniture and bric-a-brac, and tourists and locals looking to snap up a deal. The motorcycle club on your left bumps up against a warehouse for unfinished wooden furniture; across the road, a kombucha shop in a strip mall, an indicator of changing tastes in this region. Continue west, and deep front porches invite you into house after house, imposing stacks of firewood, always prepared to stave off damp rain and the long winter, alongside rockers and vintage gliders, ready for lazy summer days. To the left, through the pines, a glimpse of the vast bowl of the Ashokan Reservoir, a manmade wonder that quenches the unending thirst of New York City. A white arrow on a green road sign announces that Woodstock is just a few miles off to the right. The hills rise up ahead, the crisscross of peak against peak casting long shadows. Signs of the city slip away: you're in the Catskills now.

Around a bend, the mighty Esopus Creek comes rushing out from between the hills, moving down, down toward the Hudson. Onward are the tracks of the Catskill Mountain Railroad, a monument to the once bustling and vast network of railroads that carried people and goods—furs, produce, bluestone, dairy, lumber—up and down, east and west across the region.

A few miles farther, a towering sign that reads, simply, "Diner" rises up on your left. On a post shorter in stature, there's an artist's rendering of an old-school Woodie, the iconic American station wagon, loaded down with outdoor rec equipment—an inner tube, a canoe, skis—a nod to the long history of this road, this place, moving people toward leisure, toward a haven.

Pull in, and the parking lot is full: chrome-edged motorcycles and beat-up pickup trucks, spotless sports cars and aging station wagons packed to the gills. People come and go, chatting over coffee under the tin roof of a simple wooden pavilion where ceiling fans twirl lazily. Inside, it's the picture of a classic diner: chrome and tile, swivel stools at the counter, leather booths, paper placemats. A chalkboard announces the day's specials, and a felt letterboard above the long Formica counter advertises milkshakes, cookies, and a kids' menu: everyone is welcome here.

The kitchen hums, churning out diner standards—fried eggs, pancakes, burgers, and the like—alongside the unexpected: a skillet of soft scrambled eggs studded with smoked trout and crème fraîche, a fried catfish sandwich topped with a fish-sauced slaw, cider-braised duck over creamy grits. There's pie and pudding for dessert. At tables, long-time local residents sit side by side with Brooklyn hipsters up for the weekend, hunters sit next to vegans, and renowned musicians rub elbows with farmers. The clink of forks against ceramic and the sound of plates being scraped clean mingle with the laughter and rock and roll. No-nonsense servers offer more coffee.

It is every diner you've ever known, but the view of the mountain ridge from the plate-glass front wall and the cues on the menu—the prominence of trout; the local ramps, syrup, and cider; and a bagel with lox and cream cheese, a nod to this region's tourist past—are firm reminders that you're *here*: this is the Phoenicia Diner.

AN ACCIDENTAL
DINER OWNER

For more than twenty years, my wife, Helene, and I drove past the Phoenicia Diner on our way to our cabin, just up Route 28. The Phoenicia Diner was the sort of place you could go behind the counter and pour your own coffee. As the owners aged, though, so did the Diner. By 2011, it was in need of a makeover and was hosting only a handful of loyal local regulars, much like the Catskills region itself. As we whizzed past in the car, our two daughters tucked in the back, I often commented that someone should buy that fantastic building and bring it back to life, turn it into the destination it seemed destined to be. We never thought it would be us.

I began working in food and hospitality well into my adult life—I was fifty when I reimagined the fate of a 1962 DeRaffele Diner in Phoenicia, New York, and opened the Phoenicia Diner we have today—but the notion of bringing people together around food seeded itself in my mind way back in my childhood.

I was eight when my dad passed, suddenly leaving my mom, Marie—only thirty years old and with three young children—to fend for herself. We didn't have much in the way of money, but we had our tight-knit Italian American family around

us in Brooklyn. They supported us. To give back, Mom baked Christmas cookies, turning us kids into her elves. It became an annual event. Mom still churns out a few thousand cookies a year, with the help of my kids and their cousins. This simple act imprinted on me the desire to use food as a way of giving back to, and supporting, community.

In 2011, Hurricane Irene swept across the northeast and devastated many of the villages along the Esopus Creek. One of the afflicted towns was Phoenicia. As we drove past the Phoenicia Diner for about the thousandth time, I repeated my now old-hat refrain: "Someone should buy that place and fix up it up."

A few weeks later, we stopped in for lunch. The Diner was quiet, so I struck up a conversation with the owner, Chris Raptis, and his wife, Chrystal. Chris told me he was eighty-two, but he looked and acted decades younger; I asked to see his driver's license as proof. For more than thirty years, Chris, a Greek immigrant, had been running the place. I loved hearing about how the Diner had been transported to the Catskills on a flatbed trailer, how he ran it as a 24-hour-a-day operation for many years, and most important, about all the characters who had passed through its doors.

A week later, we shook hands on a price, and I took the reins of the Phoenicia Diner.

While the Diner was closed for renovations, we spent a lot of time considering what made sense for a restaurant in this particular community. Hurricane Irene had destroyed homes, businesses, and infrastructure in a region that had already been struggling for years. The area felt like it was in a moment of identity crisis. Some wanted to cut their losses and move on. But the optimists among us had a feeling that new life could, and should, be breathed into the region. What had always been wonderful about the Catskills was still there, after all: the wild beauty of the mountains and streams and the small towns that still operated as true communities. There was also a deep history and culture to build on—agriculture, wilderness, farming, and an openness to artistic types.

The Diner already had a lot going for it: classic architecture as well as a bang-up location. The building needed to be fixed up a bit, sure, but its bones were good. Our guiding principle was to create the kind of restaurant our customers—seasonal tourists, weekenders, and longtime locals—would want to eat at all the time.

Keeping it simple meant steering clear of the forty-page diner menus I'd flipped through as a kid and making use of the terrific food (and booze) being produced all around us. Everything would be fresh, made to order. We homed in on a select handful of diner classics, then added a few dishes that suggested we were something other than your average greasy spoon, like our Arnold Bennett Skillet (page 72)—soft scrambled eggs flecked with smoked trout and made luscious with crème fraîche—and a chile-laced tortilla soup (page 99).

After months of having the windows covered in brown paper, my wife and I cut a ribbon with the local chamber of commerce and opened the doors. No one—including me—had ever worked with a POS (point of sale) system, cooked a full menu in a freshly rebuilt kitchen, or thought to order more than six dozen eggs! Halfway through that first service, I pulled Helene aside and, with a very serious tone, said, "We have to lock the doors;

there are too many customers!" She just laughed and said, "Wipe that scared look off your face and keep smiling." We served 215 meals that day. Today, we serve four times that many meals on a busy summer day, but at the end of that first day, I cried. Let me tell you, those were *not* happy tears—they were tears of terror! What had I gotten myself into?

About four years in, by which time we'd become busier than we had ever imagined, Chef Chris Bradley joined our team. He brought with him a deep mountain sensibility, having started his cooking career in the city of Asheville, in his native North Carolina. Though he had spent nearly two decades cooking in New York, the importance of community, hard work, and the way people want to live and eat in the hills had never left him. While he was at the Diner, the food became a more definite expression of both Chris's background and our region. We came to rely more heavily than ever upon the food and drinks being produced all around us by a diverse array of people who remind us that, though the Catskills may seem remote, it's not insular. On our menu, ice cream from Ronnybrook Dairy's Hudson Valley cows sits alongside kimchi made a few valleys over by two Korean American sisters, Madalyn and Jenny Warren of Kimchee Harvest; trout pulled from our mountain lakes coexists with breakfast tacos made with Mexican-style chorizo; internationally award-winning chocolate made down the road finds its way into familiar classics like puddings, cookies, and hot chocolate.

As the Phoenicia Diner continues to grow and evolve, we build on what each team member brings to the table. They leave an indelible mark, from our Puebla-born first chef, Melchor "Mel" Rosas, to Chris Bradley and his Southern-flavor profile. It's important to the Diner's success that there will continually be varying influences on our comfort food–based menu as we welcome new kitchen management, each cook with his or her own distinct influences. It's about resourcefulness and holding one another up. It may sound a little utopian, but these hills have always been a soft landing place for the dreamers among us.

THE PHOENICIA DINER COOKBOOK

ABOUT THIS BOOK
A MISSION STATEMENT, OF SORTS

Diners have always been bastions of democracy and approachability in the ever-changing restaurant industry. They are the places where anyone can find something they will want to eat. Diners are the same everywhere, and yet each is distinct. They're recognizable by their booths and counter seating, their endless coffee refills, and menu items like eggs any way, pancakes, and classic American sandwiches. But some may have a Greek twist to their menus, sneaking in spanakopita and gyros, while others lean American Jewish, with blintzes and knishes. They're known for their no-nonsense food and sometimes salty service. From the writings of John Steinbeck to the paintings of Edward Hopper and the films of Woody Allen, in small towns and along well-traveled routes across the country, diners are an iconic, essential part of the American landscape.

They are also disappearing. One need only walk the streets of New York City's five boroughs or drive along the Main Streets of small towns to see diners shutting their doors, losing business to faceless chain restaurants or fancy coffee shops. While such establishments may follow national trends in consumer spending and dining, they tend not to fulfill the yen for local character, the sense of community and belonging, the comforting fare that diners have always offered.

Our diner, the Phoenicia Diner, is American in the broadest sense. It is also specifically *of* Phoenicia, New York, a dot on the map in a narrow valley carved by the Esopus Creek in the Catskill Mountains. This book is both a representation of our restaurant and a celebration of the community and region that supports it: its complex and fascinating history, as well as the mixture of cultures that defines it in the here and now. The blend of recipes we've featured reflects the Phoenicia Diner's culinary approach. We have familiar diner classics, of course. Then there are items that have become signatures on our menu—dishes that reflect the unique mix of cosmopolitan tastes, mountain food culture, local flavor, and, yes, a Brooklyn influence that is really the core of who we are. You'll find dishes inspired by the Catskills' history: its legacy of the "Borscht Belt" and New York City's Jewish community, the culinary imprint of the region's Native American communities, its rich dairy-producing and fruit-growing traditions, and even a nod or two to its notorious bootlegging past. Here, too, are contributions from the folks behind the scenes at the Diner, including the Mexican influence of our kitchen staff and dishes that celebrate Chef Chris's upbringing in the American South.

HOW TO SET YOURSELF UP FOR SHORT-ORDER SUCCESS (A.K.A. HOW TO USE THIS BOOK)

Part of the fun of a diner is ordering whatever you want, whenever you want—a piece of pie and a cup of coffee at seven in the morning, if you like. Tuck into a plate of eggs, potatoes, and sausage at four in the afternoon. Or make a meal of pancakes, a bowl of soup, and a milkshake. In keeping with that spirit, we've grouped the recipes to match the sorts of cravings they reflect. Cook these recipes for any time of day, in any order you like.

Good diner cooking, like good home cooking, takes time. At a restaurant where we make virtually everything from scratch, "short-order cooking" is something of a misnomer. More accurately, it's something like "short-order assembling" or "short-order finishing touches." We prep all week, every week—that is to say, continuously—baking bread, brining and curing meats, making stocks, cutting potatoes, making condiments, baking desserts, and on and on. When a busy weekend hits, our hardworking cooks might be flipping burgers at the griddle with one hand and stirring scrambled eggs with the other. But that's just the tip of the iceberg. Our cooks are able to get delicious food to our guests quickly only because the entire back-of-house team has been putting the component pieces together for hours, if not days, in advance.

At home, we recommend you take a similar approach to these recipes. As you read through this book, you'll see that some of the recipes have make-ahead components. A few are even spread out over a couple of days. Don't worry; there's no need to be intimidated. We're not asking you to work more but, rather, to work smarter. By doing a little here and there, you can break the labor into less daunting chunks, meaning you can pull many of these dishes together on a weekday or for a gathering without standing at a cutting board or over a hot stove for hours at a time.

Read through these recipes fully before you set about cooking them. Make sure you have both all the ingredients and all the time you need. Planning and prepping ahead is what makes the Diner run smoothly and efficiently, and it'll do the same for you at home.

As far as equipment goes, you won't need anything terribly specialized. A few sturdy pots and pans of various sizes are necessary, as is a good knife or two. A few recipes call for a blender, and the same goes for an electric mixer. Food processors make light work of chopping and shredding, but a box grater, a good knife, and a little patience are excellent stand-ins.

There was, of course, good cooking before most culinary appliances were invented, so there are always workarounds. (The one exception may be a waffle iron, which is really a one-trick—and irreplaceable—kitchen gadget.) Use what you've got, what you can easily borrow, and what you're comfortable with.

There is some fried food in this book. (Are you surprised? We're a diner!) While we don't want you running out to buy a home fryer, you will need a lot of oil and a candy thermometer, too. You may be tempted to skimp and make a shallower fryer than we specify in frying recipes. Don't do it! The reason deep fryers in restaurants work so well is that they have plenty of room, which helps the oil stay hot as more food is added. Overcrowding immediately lowers the temperature of the oil, and that can lead to soggy or unevenly cooked food. And if you become something of a home-frying aficionado, it makes sense to reuse your frying oil. After cooking, cool the oil completely and strain it through a fine-mesh sieve or a colander lined with cheesecloth, then transfer it to an airtight jug or a few glass jars, and store it in a cool, dark place or the fridge. Write the date on your oil each time you use it. You can get up to five rounds of frying out of the same oil, but be sure to discard it no later than six months after its original use.

When it comes to ingredients, buy the best you can find. It's what makes our food stand out, and it'll do the same for yours. In the recipe headnotes, you'll find plenty of guidance for obtaining specific ingredients. Without getting too dogmatic, here are a few general guidelines:

FRUITS AND VEGETABLES

Choose recipes for when the requisite produce is in season. (Some exceptions are storage crops like onions, garlic, potatoes, and carrots, which are easy to come by in good condition all year long. And speaking of onions, all onions are Spanish, unless otherwise noted.) We've given you notes as to which recipes rely most heavily on peak-perfect fruits and vegetables.

DAIRY

Unless otherwise noted, all dairy (milk, yogurt, cheeses, etc.) is whole fat. All butter is unsalted. Buy the freshest and best dairy products you can. If you have a local supplier making good products, support them.

EGGS

We use a lot of eggs at the Diner. A LOT. So trust us when we say that eggs matter. Short of having your own backyard chickens, a farmers market is the most reliable source for eggs. Depending upon where you live, you may have honor boxes or farmstands available. Buy the freshest eggs you can find from chickens that are allowed to, well, have a life. The cost is well worth it.

MEAT

Buying direct from livestock farmers or a very reliable butcher is your best bet. But if you can't, buy the freshest meat you can. Purchasing from a butcher counter at a supermarket—where you can select cuts—will give you more control over what you purchase than buying pre-cut and packaged meats. Besides, talking with the butcher staff often leads to helpful cooking tips.

FISH

If you purchase fresh fish, make sure it's firm and glossy, and doesn't smell of lake- or ocean-bottom muck. Fish that has been frozen immediately upon coming out of the water is a very good option and is easier to come by in many places than fresh catch. Simply defrost frozen fish overnight in the fridge before preparing.

OLIVE OIL

When it comes to olive oil, there's a lot of controversy about quality. We'll steer clear of that and simply say, if you're cooking with your olive oil, don't bother paying for the best stuff. But when it comes to finishing a dish or making a dressing, you want to use the best-quality extra-virgin olive oil you can find.

OIL FOR DEEP FRYING

At the Diner, we use vegetable oil, but peanut or safflower oil are also good options.

SALT AND PEPPER

All black pepper should be freshly ground. And unless otherwise noted, all salt is kosher salt. Buy yourself a big box, and store it in a place without too much humidity to avoid clumping. It's cheap, essential, and will last you months. Seasoning is a highly personal art, and while we give guidelines for how much to use in some recipes, when it comes to salt, tasting often is the best strategy. Season lightly, and when cooking, each time you add new ingredients to a pot or pan, add salt, trying the food as you go. Underseasoned food is a manageable fix, but oversalting can truly ruin a dish. Over time, you'll develop a feel for it.

BREAKFAST
ALL DAY

THE PHOENICIA DINER GUIDE TO
EGGS ANY WAY YOU LIKE

OVER-MEDIUM

OVER-EASY

SCRAMBLED

POACHED

HARD-BOILED

OVER-HARD

SUNNY-SIDE UP

If there's anything that makes a diner a diner, it's eggs. Lots and lots of eggs. They're the glue that holds a place like this together, the ingredient that unites the unfussy, workaday order of two sunny-side up and toast with a more sophisticated smoked trout scramble (page 72), or two delicately prepared eggs atop slow-cooked cheddar grits and fiery shrimp (page 55).

At the Phoenicia Diner, we go through upward of 750 eggs on a busy summer day—that's more than 60 dozen. The egg station is its own beast: notoriously grueling, and a true art. Eggs cook fast, and when you've got tickets streaming in for eggs cooked all manner of ways, you have to possess serious patience, dexterity, and finesse to nail each and every order. Watching a good egg cook is like watching a mixed-martial-artist-meets-dancer-meets-sleepwalker: they're so constantly in motion, and so innately attuned to what they're doing, that the cook seems to move without thinking. In short, egg cooks—especially ours—deserve a lot more credit than they get.

Lucky for you, at home you won't be short-order cooking eggs all day long. But you will be cooking eggs, and plenty of them, if you work your way through this book. When it comes to eggs, there's no substitute for practice. At the Phoenicia Diner, like in most restaurants, eggs are cooked on a flattop griddle, which gives off even and very consistent heat. At home, you likely won't be working with a griddle, but you do need to become intimately familiar with the heat levels of your burners and your egg pan of choice. Very fresh eggs also tend to cook differently from older eggs, summer eggs from free-ranging hens won't look the same as winter eggs from coop-bound birds, and farm-fresh and supermarket eggs are almost different products altogether.

All that's to say there's no exact formula for cooking eggs. But here's a basic primer to give you some guidelines.

Equipment

For all pan-cooked eggs (scrambled, sunny-side up, over-easy, -medium, and -hard), a nonstick pan is the friendliest option. A small pan works nicely for single eggs, and you'll need to scale up from there. If there's flipping involved, we don't recommend cooking more than two or three eggs at a time, as you need space to get in with a spatula.

A very well-seasoned cast-iron skillet is also a good option for scrambling, and some people won't cook an egg in any other type of pan. But if you choose cast-iron, you'll need to use extra fat in the pan to keep the eggs from sticking terribly.

For poaching and boiling, any small or medium saucepan will do.

Egg Style

FOR SCRAMBLED, crack the eggs into a bowl and use a fork or whisk with a wrist-flicking motion to whip them vigorously until the yolks and whites have come together and they're viscous and a little frothy.

Cooking time will vary tremendously based on the number of eggs you're scrambling and the size of your pan. But, in short, you want to cook scrambled eggs over medium heat, never stepping away from the pan. Heat the pan first, then add enough butter to coat the base of the pan (a teaspoon or two should be ample). Swirl the butter in the pan to distribute evenly, then pour in your eggs. Standing by and watching carefully, cook until the bottom has set (you'll see the edges turn a paler yellow) and the middle is still completely raw. Then, using a rubber spatula, pull the set egg from around the edges from the four points of the compass (that's top, bottom, left, and right sides of the pan), drawing the spatula along the bottom of the pan. Allow the eggs to cook, undisturbed, for another few seconds, just until the raw egg has begun to set around the edges, and the top is still jiggly. Then, using your spatula, fold the eggs over themselves, bringing the right side into the center, then the left side into the center, like you would an old-fashioned letter. Quickly use the spatula to poke down through the surface of the eggs, allowing the last little bit of liquid to pool out, turning off the heat immediately afterward. Turn the eggs onto a plate.

FOR SUNNY-SIDE UP, heat your pan over medium heat. When it's hot, add enough butter to coat the base of the pan. Crack your eggs on the rim of the pan—make sure to crack with conviction, as you're more likely to end up with bits of eggshell if you're tentative. Cook until the white has gone from being translucent to opaque—you shouldn't see any clear gel floating atop the white—and the outer rim of the yolk has turned just a shade paler than it was raw. Use a rubber spatula to loosen the edges of the white and slide up under the center of the eggs, being sure it's not stuck. Slide the eggs onto a plate.

FOR OVER-EASY, begin the same way as you do for a sunny-side up egg. Cook the eggs only until the outer half of the white has turned from translucent to opaque and the inner half still has plenty of clear, uncooked white on top. Using a rubber spatula, working quickly, loosen all the way around the edges and make sure you can get a spatula up underneath the center of the eggs. Now comes the flipping. There's no debate here—the best way to flip a fried egg is with a quick jerking of the wrist, launching the eggs into the air and landing them back into the pan on the other side. This takes practice, plenty of broken eggs, and a hefty dose of confidence (even if you're faking it). If you're tentative at all here, your egg won't catch enough air, and you'll get a half-flipped egg that falls back in on itself. Give it a go. You'll get it soon enough. For over-easy eggs, once you've flipped, take the eggs off the heat, and allow them to sit in the hot pan another 3 to 4 seconds just so the bottom sets, then immediately slide the eggs out of the pan. When you poke gently at the yolk, it'll keep its shape but be very soft, like the chub around a baby's wrist. When you cut it open, the yolk should ooze out.

FOR OVER-MEDIUM, follow the same steps as over-easy, but allow the eggs to sit in the hot pan 15 to 20 seconds. When you poke gently at the yolk, it should feel slightly firm but give under pressure, like a ripe peach. When you cut it open, the center of the yolk will still ooze out, but some set, paler yellow yolk will still cling to the white. Slide out of the pan immediately.

FOR OVER-HARD, begin as you would for sunny-side up eggs. Once the white has set slightly, use the tip of the rubber spatula to break the yolk. Then flip the egg, leaving the heat on this time, and cooking until the egg is firm throughout and the yolk is fully set, 10 to 12 seconds. Slide out of the pan immediately.

FOR POACHED, you need a little practice. Have your eggs at the ready, right next to your pan. Fill a medium saucepan with 4 to 6 inches of water. Over high heat, bring the water to a rolling boil. Add 2 tablespoons of distilled white vinegar. Lower the heat to medium-low so the water comes to a gentle simmer, with just a few bubbles occasionally rising to the surface. Using a spoon, stir vigorously around the edges to create a whirlpool in the center. Once it gets going, crack one egg and gently drop it directly into the center of the whirlpool. Cook 3 minutes, no more and no less, until the white has gone completely opaque. Hold a kitchen towel in one hand and a slotted spoon in another, and use the spoon to remove the egg from the water. Gently dab the bottom of the spoon with the towel to dry up any excess water. Serve immediately.

FOR HARD-BOILED: We use a lot of these at the Diner. While we don't get many calls for hard-boiled eggs on a breakfast plate, we often add them to salads and toasts. They make for quick, easy, and cheap protein; they look elegant sliced on an open-faced sandwich; and they are terrific packed, whole, into a backpack for a snack on the go. There are many ways to boil an egg, but we swear by this one. Bring a medium saucepan of water to a rolling boil over high heat. Gently lower in the eggs one at a time. Let the water come back to a boil and set your timer for 11 minutes, then immediately turn the heat down to a medium simmer, so the water is just gently bubbling and the eggs are just barely burbling around in the pot. Have a slotted spoon at the ready. When the timer goes off, use the spoon to quickly remove the eggs from the pot. Serve hot and whole, or lower into a bowl of cold water and ice and allow the eggs to cool at least 10 minutes. Keep whole and unpeeled in the fridge until ready to eat. Peel the eggs under cool running water.

Ingredients

8 corn **tortillas**

8 ounces **Mexican chorizo**

8 large **eggs**

1 cup shredded **sharp cheddar cheese** (white or yellow)

1 small **romaine heart**, shredded

2 large (beefsteak) ripe **tomatoes**, cored, quartered, seeded, and diced

½ cup crumbled **queso fresco**

Salsa Verde, for serving (recipe follows)

BREAKFAST TACOS
WITH CHORIZO AND SALSA VERDE

Serves 4

These tacos are a perpetual favorite at the Diner. Filled with crisped chorizo, scrambled eggs, and two kinds of cheese, they're hearty enough to fuel a hike or replenish you after a day on the ski slopes. Like much of the best Mexican-inspired cooking, the richness of meat and dairy here is tempered with bright, fresh toppings—crunchy romaine, sweetly acidic tomatoes, and piquant salsa verde.

Make sure you're using fresh Mexican-style chorizo rather than dried Spanish-style chorizo. If your chorizo comes stuffed into sausage casings, simply slice down the length of the casing using the tip of a sharp knife and pull the sausage meat loose using the edge of a metal spoon.

You want the salsa verde to cool and its flavors to come together before serving, so it's best to make it the morning or even the night before you plan to serve. Double the salsa recipe if you want to have extra around for dipping or dolloping.

1. Lightly toast each tortilla over the low flame of a gas burner, on a grill, or in a warm pan for 10 to 15 seconds on each side. When the tortillas are slightly charred and pliant, wrap them in a kitchen towel to keep warm and prevent them from drying out.

2. Heat a large nonstick pan over high heat. Place the chorizo in the pan and cook, undisturbed, until brown and crispy, about 5 minutes. Lower the heat to medium and use a wooden spoon to break the chorizo up into crumbles. If there is an excessive amount of grease released by the chorizo, drain all but 1 tablespoon.

3. Crack the eggs into a mixing bowl and beat with a fork or whisk until they are thoroughly blended. Add the eggs to the pan of chorizo and cook over medium heat, using a rubber spatula or wooden spoon to stir occasionally. Continue cooking until the eggs are set but still soft and fluffy, 2 to 3 minutes. Turn off the heat and sprinkle the cheddar cheese over the eggs, then gently fold everything together.

4. Place the tortillas on plates or a platter and evenly divide the egg and chorizo mixture among them. Top each tortilla with chopped romaine, diced tomatoes, and queso fresco. Serve with Salsa Verde on the side (serving with the salsa on top leads to almost immediately soggy tacos), giving it a quick stir before spooning it over the top of the tacos when you sit down to eat, as it may have separated some while cooling.

RECIPE CONTINUES ➤➤

Salsa Verde

Makes about 1 cup

8 ounces ripe **tomatillos** (4 to 5 large), husked and rinsed

1 **jalapeño pepper**, stemmed (if you prefer a less spicy salsa, remove the core and seeds from the chile)

1 **garlic clove**

Kosher salt

¼ cup chopped **fresh cilantro**

2 tablespoons fresh **lime juice**

1. Place the tomatillos, jalapeño, and garlic in a medium saucepan, and add a heavy pinch of kosher salt and enough water just to cover. Bring the water to a boil over high heat. Cook, uncovered, until the tomatillos are fork-tender, 7 to 8 minutes.

2. Use a slotted spoon to transfer the tomatillos, jalapeño, and garlic to a blender. Add the cilantro and lime juice, and blend until smooth. Season the salsa with additional salt to taste and place in a container in the refrigerator. (The salsa will keep, refrigerated, for up to 1 week.)

BUTTERMILK BISCUITS AND SAUSAGE GRAVY

Serves 8

Biscuits and gravy are a study in contrast: fluffy biscuits, flaky on the inside and crispy around the edges, topped with a thick, rich, meaty gravy. The dish was developed as the breakfast of working folk, eaten after early morning chores were done to fortify them through the rest of the morning's labors. Most of us don't quite live that way anymore, but there's still a place for a true country breakfast like this one. Just don't make any plans other than a nap after a big plate of these.

1. Position a rack in the center of the oven and preheat the oven to 400°F.

2. **Make the biscuits:** Into a large bowl, sift together the flour, baking powder, baking soda, and salt. Set a box grater directly onto the flour mixture, its base resting in the flour. Working quickly and using the largest holes of the grater, grate the frozen butter into the flour. Then use your hands to gently knead the butter into the flour just until it takes on the texture of coarse crumbs.

3. Make a well in the center of the mixture. Add the buttermilk to the well and use a wooden spoon to pull scoops of flour into the well of buttermilk in the center until the dough just comes together (don't be tempted to do any extra mixing, as you don't want to overwork the dough). Continue until all the flour has been incorporated; the dough should be a bit wet but not too sticky. Press the dough together into a rough ball, dipping your hands in flour if you find the dough is sticking to your skin.

4. Generously dust a work surface with flour. Turn the dough out and press it into a flat rectangle roughly 1 inch thick. Brush off any excess flour from the top of the dough, then gently fold it in half and press down again into the same shape and size.

5. Use a 3½-inch biscuit cutter or round drinking glass (the mouth of a canning jar works nicely, too) to cut the biscuits, leaving at least ⅛ inch between each cut. Press the cutter straight down into the dough (twisting will pinch the edges of the biscuits and prevent them from properly rising), wiping the cutter clean and dipping it into the flour after every few cuts. Without overworking the dough, gather the scraps together and press them out again into a 1-inch-thick rectangle. Repeat the process (you should end up with 8 to 10 biscuits).

RECIPE CONTINUES ➺

4 cups **all-purpose flour**, plus more for dusting

2 tablespoons **baking powder**

2 teaspoons **baking soda**

1 tablespoon **kosher salt**

¾ cup (1½ sticks) **unsalted butter**, frozen

2 cups **buttermilk**

FOR THE SAUSAGE GRAVY

1 pound bulk **breakfast sausage** (see Note, page 35)

4 tablespoons (½ stick) **unsalted butter**

½ cup **all-purpose flour**

4 cups **whole milk**

1 cup **buttermilk**

1 teaspoon **kosher salt**

1 teaspoon freshly ground **black pepper**

6. Place the biscuits on an unlined baking sheet and bake, rotating once halfway through, until they are fluffy, the base is dark golden brown, and the tops have just turned a pale gold, 10 to 15 minutes.

7. Meanwhile, make the sausage gravy: Heat a large heavy-bottomed saucepan over medium-high heat. Add the sausage and cook, stirring occasionally to break it up into small marble-size pieces, until it's browned and has released its fat, about 10 minutes. (By this time, your biscuits should be ready—pull them from the oven and allow them to cool slightly.)

8. Add the butter to the pan and stir it around to melt. Scrape the bottom of the pan to loosen any browned bits of sausage. Sprinkle the flour over the sausage while stirring constantly. Cook, continuing to stir constantly, until all the flour has been incorporated into the fat and is sandy brown, just a minute or two.

9. Carefully pour in the whole milk and buttermilk, stirring constantly, just until the mixture starts to bubble. Immediately reduce the heat to medium-low and season with the salt and pepper. Continue to simmer, stirring occasionally to avoid burning on the bottom, until the gravy is velvety, thick enough to uniformly coat a spoon, and no longer has a flavor of raw flour, 12 to 15 minutes (see Note).

10. The biscuits are now ready to meet the gravy. Serve them whole on plates or split them in half, smother the warm biscuits, or stuff their middles full with gravy. You can't go wrong.

NOTES: Bulk sausage—loose sausage that hasn't been stuffed into a casing—was once a mainstay, available at butcher shops and even most grocery stores. But if you're having trouble finding it, you can purchase uncooked breakfast sausages and simply cut the fillings out of their casings.

If the gravy is too thick for your liking, add a little milk or buttermilk at the end. Additionally, depending on the type of sausage you use, you may want to add more or less salt, pepper, or other spices (such as ground sage, ground ginger, marjoram, or chile flakes).

PERFECT BACON, EGG, AND CHEESE

Serves 1

2 slices **bacon**

2 large **eggs**

Kosher salt and freshly ground **black pepper**

1 **Kaiser roll** (we use unseeded), sliced

About 2 tablespoons **unsalted butter**

2 tablespoons shredded **sharp white cheddar cheese**

Hot sauce, **ketchup**, **mayo**, or **tomato slices**, for serving (optional)

The bacon, egg, and cheese is one of those iconic New York City foods. Every bodega and short-order deli in the city slings these simple, just-greasy-enough breakfast sandwiches. They're oh-so-satisfying, and the perfect hangover cure to boot.

At the Diner, we serve ours straight from the griddle, unwrapped, like any other sandwich. But to replicate that bodega experience, as soon as your sandwich is assembled, wrap it in aluminum foil to allow all the component parts to steam together into a more cohesive, gooey whole.

. . . .

1. In a heavy skillet over medium heat, cook the bacon to your liking. Lay the bacon on paper towels to drain, then break each slice in half so you have four pieces. Wipe out the pan with a paper towel, then return to the stove over medium heat. Meanwhile, crack your eggs into a bowl, season lightly with salt and pepper, and whisk until smooth. Set aside.

2. Slather each half of the roll with about half a tablespoon of butter, then lay it in the hot skillet until it has developed a golden crust. Remove the roll halves from the pan, wiping out any remnants with a paper towel, and return the skillet to the stove over medium heat. Lay the bacon on one half of the roll.

3. Heat the remaining butter in the pan, then pour your eggs into the hot pan. Using a spatula, stir them a bit, until the bottom just sets. Use the spatula to loosen around the edges, then flip the eggs over. Turn the heat off, sprinkle the cheese across the surface, and fold the eggs in half—like an omelet—and allow the residual heat to finish cooking the eggs just until softly set.

4. Slide the eggs onto the bacon on the roll and add the condiments of your choice. Top with the remaining roll half and either wrap the sandwich in foil or eat immediately.

NOTE: These quantities are for a single sandwich, but you can easily feed a crowd by scaling up, keeping the proportions the same.

THE PHOENICIA DINER GUIDE TO BACON DONE RIGHT

At the Diner, we go through anywhere from 150 to 200 pounds of bacon in a busy week. So we get a lot of practice cooking the stuff. While cooking bacon in a skillet for one or two people is perfectly respectable, if you're nervous about overcooking or feeding a crowd, here's a foolproof method:

Preheat the oven to 375°F. Line a rimmed baking sheet with foil and a large plate or two with a double layer of paper towels.

Lay the bacon on the baking sheet in a single layer—the slices can touch, but don't let them overlap. Cook the bacon for 8 minutes. Remove the baking sheet from the oven and use a fork to flip the bacon slices. (If the bacon is swimming in hot grease at this point, go ahead and pour off the fat into a throwaway container, glass jar, or clean tin can for later use.) Slide the bacon back into the oven and cook until the meat of the bacon is reddish brown and the fat has turned a pale beige color, another 5 to 6 minutes. There will be hot liquid fat that has rendered out into the pan, and the bacon won't be super crispy yet; don't worry, the crisping up happens when the excess fat has drained off and the bacon has had a chance to cool a bit.

Transfer the bacon to the paper towel–lined plate and allow to cool and drain for a couple of minutes before serving.

SMOKED TROUT BAGELS
WITH SCALLION CREAM CHEESE

Serves 4

New York's distinct Eastern European Jewish food culture has long had a strong influence on the Catskills region. In the mid-twentieth century, many of the grand Catskills resorts—the subset known as "The Borscht Belt"—catered to New York Jews, enticing them away from the city with fresh air and cooler temperatures, so as to kick back and socialize. If you've seen the show *The Marvelous Mrs. Maisel*, you've caught a glimpse into this world of summers past.

Perusing menus from these resorts is like finding a time capsule of the Lower East Side and Brooklyn of yore, replete with the smoked fish and creamy spreads—lox, cream cheese, whitefish salad, pickled herring—you would find in the appetizing shops of those neighborhoods. While the grand resorts are gone now, the cultural link between the Catskills and New York City is still strong. This version of the fully loaded classic bagel—heftily schmeared with cream cheese and topped with smoked fish—feeds our hankering for New York's iconic foods. Here, we showcase local smoked trout, a regional specialty.

1. Put the cream cheese in a medium bowl. Add the scallions, horseradish, lemon zest and juice, and a sprinkling each of salt and pepper. Stir vigorously with a wooden spoon until all the ingredients are well blended.

2. Spread a generous amount of the cream cheese on each toasted bagel half, reserving any leftover for later use. Sprinkle the capers over the cream cheese.

3. Check the trout fillets for bones and skin, then break the fillets into finger-length pieces. Lay the fish evenly across the bagel halves. Garnish each sandwich with a lettuce leaf, tomato slice, and onion slice and finish with the bagel top, then serve.

1 cup (8 ounces, or 1 standard block) **cream cheese**, softened

¼ cup thinly sliced **scallions**, green and white parts (2 to 4 scallions, depending on thickness)

1 tablespoon prepared **horseradish**

Zest and juice of 1 **lemon**

Kosher salt and freshly ground **black pepper**

4 **bagels**, sliced in half and toasted (see Note)

4 tablespoons drained **capers**

2 fillets of **smoked trout**

4 large **lettuce leaves**, such as green leaf, red oak, Bibb, or romaine, washed and dried

4 slices perfectly ripe **tomato**

1 small **red onion**, thinly sliced

NOTE: It goes without saying that a really good bagel makes all the difference, so use the best you have access to, and buy them fresh—ideally, the same day you'll be serving them.

8 large **Yukon Gold potatoes** (about 4 pounds; see Note)

¼ cup **olive oil**

Kosher salt

Vegetable oil, for frying

Rosemary Salt (recipe follows)

PHOENICIAN POTATOES
WITH ROSEMARY SALT

Serves 4, generously, as a side

A diner must have a potato side dish. Must. These are ours. Not a traditional home fry per se, but, in our opinion, the quintessential side potato. The trick here is double-cooking the potatoes: first roasting and then frying them. The roasting slow-cooks the potatoes on the inside and the high heat of the fryer finishes them with an ultra-crispy skin on the outside.

The rosemary salt recipe we provide here makes more than you'll need for a single batch of potatoes, but you'll find it's a useful addition to your pantry. Rosemary salt is the key to flavoring these potatoes; we also use it as the seasoning base to make several of our skillets unique. It's a terrific seasoning for roast vegetables and meats. When it comes to making the herb salt, feel free to scale the recipe up; once you've got a batch, it keeps almost indefinitely in your spice drawer—the salt effectively dehydrating and preserving the rosemary leaves—and can be used to season all manner of meats and vegetables bound for roasting.

1. Preheat the oven to 350°F.

2. Cut the potatoes into 1-inch cubes and place in a large mixing bowl. Toss with the olive oil and about a tablespoon of kosher salt. Place the potatoes in a single even layer on a baking sheet (if needed, use more than one sheet; the potatoes can touch, but don't let them overlap). Roast, without stirring, until tender but not completely soft, about 30 minutes. If using more than one sheet on different racks in your oven, rotate the sheets halfway through to make sure they cook evenly. Set the potatoes aside to cool.

3. Fill a Dutch oven or other deep pot with 4 inches of oil (see tips on home frying, page 19). Heat to 375°F (a candy thermometer works well here) over high heat. Working in batches, add the potatoes, making sure the oil doesn't spill over the top. Fry, undisturbed, until deep golden brown, 3 to 4 minutes.

4. Using a slotted spoon, remove the potatoes from the pan, shaking gently to drip off extra fat, and transfer to a bowl. Season generously with the rosemary salt and serve.

NOTE: Make sure you use waxy Yukon Gold potatoes here, which are able to stand up to the one-two punch of roasting and frying.

Rosemary Salt

Makes ½ cup

4 sprigs of **fresh rosemary**, leaves picked off
(1 heaping tablespoon leaves)

½ cup **kosher salt**

1. Place the rosemary leaves between 2 paper towels on a plate. Place the plate in a microwave and cook on high for 1 minute. Rotate the plate if needed and microwave again for 15 more seconds. (Alternatively, you can deep-fry the rosemary, woody stems and all, then strip the leaves from the stems once the rosemary has cooled.)

2. Place the dried rosemary and the salt in a spice or coffee grinder and grind until thoroughly blended. Use immediately or store in an airtight container in a cool, dark place. Keeps (almost) indefinitely.

THE PHOENICIA DINER GUIDE TO
THE FULL PHOENICIAN BREAKFAST

This is our riff on a full English breakfast, the sort you see all over the UK, from roadside eateries to white-tablecloth restaurants. While traditionally this is a meat-heavy meal, there's lots of room for personalization here: swap sautéed mushrooms for bacon, or a turkey sausage patty in lieu of pork sausage.

While homemade baked beans are delicious, we use canned beans here: this breakfast isn't meant to be a huge production, but rather a quick assembly for a hardy start to your day. There are several good-quality brands of baked beans on the market, and they vary widely from region to region. Hunts and Bush's are readily available throughout the country and are reliably high quality. We like beans flavored with pork, but by all means use vegetarian baked beans if you're avoiding meat.

These are assembly instructions more than they are a recipe. Have a warm (200°F) oven and 2 baking sheets—one lined with paper towels—at the ready.

Spread 1 cup Phoenician Potatoes with Rosemary Salt (page 42) evenly across one of the baking sheets and put in the oven to warm.

In a heavy-bottomed skillet over medium heat, cook 3 slices of bacon to your liking. Lay the bacon onto the paper towels on the tray, and slide into the oven to keep warm. Pour off the bacon fat and discard or reserve to cook your eggs.

In the same skillet over medium heat, cook 1 breakfast sausage link until all the pink is gone from the center and the outer casing has developed a taut, brown sheen. Wipe out the skillet and set back on the stove over high heat.

While the pan heats back up, pour ½ cup of baked beans into a small saucepan and set to warm over low heat. Meanwhile, cut 2 thick slices off a ripe tomato.

When a flick of water dropped into the skillet instantly sizzles away, lay the tomato slices into the pan, side by side. Cook them just long enough to warm through and develop some good brown color, about 1 minute, then flip with a spatula and repeat on the other side. Add the tomatoes to the baking sheet in the oven, then wipe any tomato remnants from the pan and return it to the stove over medium heat.

Pop a slice or two of your favorite bread into the toaster. Meanwhile, assemble all the breakfast components on a large plate, buttering your toast while it's still warm.

Cook 2 eggs any way you like them in your skillet (see pages 28–29), add them to your plate, and tuck in immediately.

COUNTRY-FRIED STEAK AND EGGS

Serves 4

The name "country-fried steak" can raise a lot of eyebrows in these parts: What is it, exactly? And why would you bread and fry a perfectly good steak? The answer requires looking back a ways, to German immigrants in the American South, who brought with them *Wiener schnitzel*, their traditional way of pounding meat (veal, specifically) into thin cutlets, then breading and frying them to delicious effect. Like its German predecessor, country-fried steak makes use of a tougher cut of meat, tenderizing it by pounding. The thin cutlets are given a quick dredge, then swiftly pan-fried. The crowning glory is the gravy, which picks up all the flavorful bits left in the pan and gives them new life.

FOR THE STEAKS

4 (6-ounce) **top round or sirloin tip steaks**

1 cup **cornstarch** (see Note)

2 large **eggs**

½ cup **buttermilk**

1 cup **all-purpose flour**

½ teaspoon **smoked paprika**

1 teaspoon **kosher salt**, plus more to taste

1 teaspoon freshly ground **black pepper**, plus more to taste

2 cups **canola oil**

FOR THE GRAVY

3 tablespoons **unsalted butter**

¼ cup **all-purpose flour**

1½ cups **whole milk**

½ cup **buttermilk**

1 tablespoon freshly ground **black pepper**

Kosher salt

FOR SERVING

8 large **eggs**, cooked to your liking (see pages 28–29)

Phoenician Potatoes with Rosemary Salt (page 42; see Note)

1. **Prepare the steaks:** Place one of the steaks in a plastic storage bag or between 2 sheets of wax paper and use a meat mallet or small skillet to pound the steak to approximately a ⅛-inch thickness. Repeat this process with the remaining steaks. Place the steaks in the fridge to chill, at least 10 minutes, or up to overnight.

2. Place the cornstarch in a shallow dish. Place the eggs and buttermilk together in another shallow dish and whisk until combined. Place the flour, paprika, 1 teaspoon salt, and 1 teaspoon black pepper in a third shallow dish and whisk until the seasoning is thoroughly mixed into the flour.

3. Working one at a time, season the steaks with salt and pepper. Dip each steak first into the cornstarch, turning to fully coat both sides, then shake off any excess cornstarch (there will be leftover cornstarch in the dish). Dip the steak into the egg and buttermilk mixture, using a fork to lift the steak out of the dish and allow any excess egg to run off. Finally, dredge the steak in the flour mixture, turning to evenly coat both sides, again shaking off any excess flour. Place the breaded steaks on a clean plate, then put them back into the fridge to keep cool.

4. Preheat the oven to 200°F and have a baking sheet or large platter at the ready.

5. In a large cast-iron skillet over medium-high heat, bring the canola oil to 375°F. Working one at a time, carefully place a steak into the skillet and cook until golden brown on the bottom, about 2 to 3 minutes. Use a fork or metal spatula to turn the steak over and cook until the other

side is brown, an additional 1 to 2 minutes. Remove the steak to a paper towel–lined plate and repeat with the remaining steaks. (If your cast-iron skillet is large enough to accommodate more than one steak at a time without overlapping, feel free to double up.)

6. Once all the steaks are browned, turn off the heat and allow the oil to cool, 10 to 15 minutes. Carefully pour off the oil from the pan, trying to save as many of the crusty browned bits on the bottom as possible.

7. Make the gravy: Return the pan to medium-high heat and melt the butter until it begins to bubble. Add the flour and use a wooden spoon to vigorously stir the butter and flour together. Cook the roux until it has darkened to the color of light caramel and has the texture of heavy, wet sand, about 2 minutes. Slowly pour in the whole milk while continuously whisking to make sure any clumps of roux are incorporated. Increase the heat to high and allow the gravy to come to a boil for about 1 minute while continuing to whisk. Reduce the heat to a low simmer and whisk in the buttermilk, black pepper, and salt to taste. Continue to cook, occasionally stirring, until the gravy has thickened and generously coats the back of a spoon, about 5 minutes.

8. Place each steak on a plate and smother with a generous helping of gravy, 2 cooked eggs, and a mound of potatoes. Serve immediately.

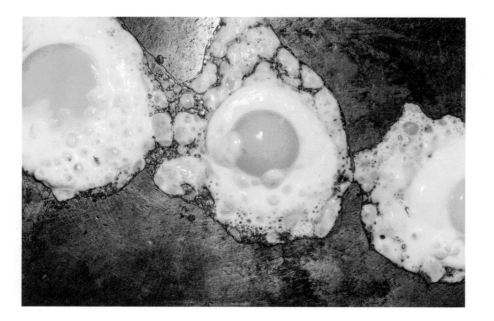

NOTES: We call for a cup of cornstarch here, which is more than the steaks will actually need for dredging. When breading, you always want extra in the dish to ensure ample and even coating.

Have your Phoenician Potatoes ready to go and kept warm in the oven before you start on the steaks.

STEAK CHILAQUILES
WITH SALSA ROJA
Serves 4

1 pound **flank steak**, cut into 4 (4-ounce) pieces

Kosher salt and freshly ground **black pepper**

1 tablespoon **ancho chile powder**

Salsa Roja (recipe follows; see Note)

10 cups **corn tortilla chips** (about 12 ounces; see Note)

1 ripe **avocado**, sliced

1 small **red onion**, sliced into thin half-moons (about 1 cup)

¼ cup chopped **fresh cilantro**

4 large **eggs**

2 **limes**, cut into 4 wedges each

Chilaquile comes from the word for chiles and greens in the Aztec ancient language, Nahuatl, which is still spoken in pockets of central Mexico. Though its roots are ancient and a little romantic sounding, chilaquiles are just commonsense, economical home cooking. It's an inexpensive and filling dish that helps use up bits and bobs commonly found in the Mexican pantry: corn tortillas that have started to go stale, a single lime, a few eggs, an onion, a tomato, and a handful of stray chiles. Here, we add some heft to the dish with steak, making for a Mexican-inspired take on steak and eggs.

While restaurants often serve chilaquiles made with tangy salsa verde, at the Diner we like ours with a deep, fiery Salsa Roja. It's satisfying, salty, and quite spicy—in short, perfect hangover food.

1. Heat a grill or grill pan over high heat until smoking hot. Meanwhile, season the steaks on both sides with a couple pinches of salt, black pepper, and the ancho chile powder. Cook the steaks to medium rare, 3 to 5 minutes on each side, depending on the thickness of your steak. Remove from the heat and let the steaks rest while you prepare the chips.

2. In a large skillet, pour half the salsa, heating it over medium heat until the sauce just reaches a low simmer. Add half the chips, cooking 2 to 3 minutes, just until the chips soften. Transfer to a large platter or baking sheet, and repeat with the rest of the salsa and chips.

3. Lay out 4 large plates, divvying up the chips evenly among them. Slice the steak. Top the chips with the avocado, red onion, cilantro, and steak slices.

4. Finally, fry up your eggs (we make them sunny-side up for this dish, but feel free to cook them as you prefer— see pages 28–29), and slide an egg onto each serving. Serve immediately, with 2 lime wedges apiece.

Salsa Roja

Makes about 3½ cups

1 **dried ancho chile** (see Note)

3 **dried guajillo chiles**

3 **dried costeno chiles**

1 **chile de árbol** (omit if you want a milder salsa)

1 large **onion**, cut into 1-inch-thick rings

1 large (beefsteak) ripe **tomato**

1 tablespoon **vegetable oil**

3 **garlic cloves**

1 teaspoon ground **cumin**

1 teaspoon freshly ground **black pepper**

1 teaspoon **kosher salt**

1 tablespoon fresh **lime juice**

1. Bring a medium saucepan (at least 4 cups) of water to a boil. Meanwhile, put the chiles into a large heatproof bowl. Once the water has come to a boil, remove the pan from the heat and pour the water over the chiles. Cover the bowl with a plate, and allow to sit for 30 minutes.

2. While the chiles are soaking, prepare the onion rings and whole tomato. Heat a grill or grill pan (if you don't have either, you can use a cast-iron skillet to similar effect)—you want it smoking hot. Drizzle the onion rings and tomato with the oil. Lay the onions on the grill and leave, undisturbed, for 5 minutes on each side, until softened and well charred along the edges (in a 400°F oven, simply leave the vegetables alone and let them cook for about 20 minutes).

3. Drain the peppers in a colander. Pull out the pepper stems and scrape the seeds from the insides (don't worry if there are a few clingers-on). In a blender, combine the soaked chiles, onion rings, tomato, garlic, cumin, pepper, salt, and lime juice. Add ½ cup water and whizz on high until very smooth; the salsa will have the texture of loose tomato sauce. (Salsa Roja will keep, tightly covered in the refrigerator, for up to 1 week.)

NOTES: Dried chiles are excellent pantry staples to have around for making flavorful salsas and adding depth and, yes, sometimes heat to soups and stews. They're increasingly available in supermarkets, particularly in urban areas, but if you can't find them at yours, they're easily purchased online (and quite affordable). Kept in a dark, cool place in an airtight container, they last for up to a year (date them!); after that, it's best to discard and replace.

Make the salsa a day ahead to allow its flavor to mellow slightly before serving.

We recommend buying the best-quality corn tortilla chips you can find at your local supermarket (look for a bit of thickness so they can hold up to the weight of the salsa). But if you're feeling particularly ambitious, you can fry your own corn chips, like we do at the Diner. Use 16 corn tortillas, cut into chip-size wedges, fried in a deep fryer for a couple of minutes—just until they're lightly browned—then drain well on paper towels or a brown paper bag.

THE PHOENICIA DINER GUIDE TO THE GLORY OF GRITS

Even as a son of the American South—the land of grits, if ever there was one—Chef Chris didn't taste real grits until the late '90s, when he was several years into his professional cooking career. When he became the executive chef of the Market Place in Asheville, North Carolina—a pioneer in that community's farm-to-table dining scene—grits were on the menu. Given his childhood associations (he was accustomed to instant grits, which reminded him of wet sawdust), he was surprised to see them in a white-tablecloth establishment. There, grits spoke of place, and spoke well. *True* grits are a revelation. They're warm and filling, tasting distinctly of themselves and smelling like row upon row of field corn in Indian summer, the essence of dried corn husks in the warm sun.

At the Diner, we use Anson Mills Antebellum Coarse White Grits. Anson Mills products are both widely available by mail order and very reliable in terms of flavor (they ship their grits frozen, which keeps the ground corn from going rancid and the superb corny flavor from depleting). If you order them for home cooking, make sure to store the grits in your freezer. Smaller, regional grain milling operations are having something of a revival, but they tend to retail only regionally. Scope out your options and, if you find something milled in small batches near you, go for it; you'll likely be rewarded with superior corn flavor. For our Classic Cheddar Grits recipe, which forms the basis of many other dishes (pages 55, 56, 58, 80, and 89), if all you can find are yellow grits, feel free to use them.

Our grits can be prepared up to 2 days ahead; made much more ahead than that, they'll go sour, owing to the cooked and then recooled milk. Store them in an airtight container in the fridge.

If you've prepared the grits ahead of time, simply warm them in a saucepan over low heat with half a cup of water or whole milk, whisking frequently. When they've begun to loosen up, increase the heat to medium, whisking constantly to avoid burning. Cook until they're smooth and creamy and burbling slightly. If the grits are still lumpy and a bit dry, add another 2 tablespoons of liquid at a time, waiting until fully absorbed after each addition before adding any more.

You'll notice that we use fine sea salt rather than kosher salt for our grits. With a dish as elemental as grits, the quality and flavor of each ingredient is crucial, and the minerality and salinity of sea salt are good bedfellows with the earthiness of dried corn.

CLASSIC CHEDDAR GRITS

Makes about 5 cups

The world of instant grits tricked Americans into thinking grits are a quick, easy, and bland breakfast item, like 5-minute oatmeal. Not so. Know that these aren't *those* grits. *These* grits are creamy, savory, and deeply satisfying all on their own, and they make a terrific base for all sorts of things (you'll find plenty of suggestions in this book).

Real grits take time and patience, but not much else. Learn to wait and trust low heat, and you'll be delighted with the results. Our grits are an overnight affair, so plan accordingly.

For storage and reheating instructions, see the opposite page.

1 cup **coarse-ground grits**

2 cups **whole milk**

1 teaspoon **fine sea salt**

1 cup grated **aged white cheddar cheese**

1 tablespoon **unsalted butter**

Freshly ground **black pepper**

1. In a heavy-bottomed pot, combine the grits and 2 cups water and gently stir a few times with a wooden spoon. Skim off any bits of hull or chaff that float to the top, then cover and leave to soak at room temperature at least 8 hours, or overnight.

2. In the morning, add the milk to the pot and cook over medium-high heat, stirring constantly to keep the milk and grits from sticking to the bottom, until the grits begin to thicken and bubble, 7 to 10 minutes. Reduce the heat to the lowest setting possible and cover. Cook, uncovering only to stir every 20 minutes or so, until the grits appear smooth and creamy, but fairly firm. This can take anywhere from 30 minutes to

1 hour, depending on what "low" is like on your range, and whether you're working over gas or electric heat. If the grits seem a bit dry (chunky rather than lusciously smooth), add as much as another ½ cup of milk, in 2 tablespoon increments, and cook for another 10 to 15 minutes until the grits have smoothed and absorbed all the additional liquid.

3. When the grits are fully cooked and at the right consistency, add the salt, cheddar, and butter and stir until incorporated. Remove from the heat and serve immediately, topped with a few turns from a pepper mill.

K-TOWN SHRIMP AND GRITS

Serves 4

This is the kind of cultural mash-up you might expect to find in some hip urban restaurant, but the components are, in fact, perfect diner fodder. Shrimp and grits was first developed in the American South as an economical way to get fishermen on their way in the wee hours—the grits already cooked on the stove, the shrimp requiring only a couple of minutes in a hot pan. Our Korean twist on the dish came about when Madalyn Warren, a local kimchi maker, dropped off samples of her wares at the Diner one day. She brought kimchi of all stripes: classic napa cabbage, garlic scape, and even rhubarb. Kimchi, a condiment first developed as a way of preserving vegetables without refrigeration, squared with the Diner ethos of humble home cooking elevated, just slightly, for a restaurant menu. While kimchi is more commonly seen served with rice or noodles, Chef Chris found that it works extremely well with our cheddar grits, acting as a foil for their richness with its signature tang and heat.

We recommend using napa cabbage kimchi here, as it's the easiest to find in stores. But if you have a favorite kimchi that spotlights another main ingredient, by all means substitute it.

Remember, the grits and pork belly both require some advance preparation, so get them going the day before you plan to serve this dish.

1 tablespoon **vegetable oil**

Cured Pork Belly (page 83), cut into ½-inch cubes

12 **jumbo shrimp**, peeled and deveined (about 8 ounces)

2 cups chopped **napa cabbage kimchi**

Classic Cheddar Grits (page 53), warmed

4 large **eggs**

4 **scallions**, green and white parts, thinly sliced

Freshly ground **black pepper**

Hot sauce, for serving (optional)

1. Heat a large cast-iron skillet over high heat. Pour the oil in the pan and add the pork belly. Cook for 4 or 5 minutes, stirring occasionally to ensure the pork gets evenly browned and is crispy on all sides. With the pork belly still in the pan, carefully drain off all but 2 tablespoons of the fat. Return the pan to the stove.

2. Add the shrimp, moving them around to make sure each lies flat and makes contact with the bottom of the pan. Cook over high heat until they've taken on some color, begun to lose their translucency, and firmed up a bit, about 3 minutes, then carefully turn them over. Cook for another 1 to 2 minutes, until the other side has browned slightly. Add the kimchi to the pan, quickly stirring to combine everything before removing from the heat.

3. Divide the grits among 4 warm bowls. Spoon the pork belly and shrimp mixture over the top.

4. Cook the eggs sunny-side up (see page 29), and slide one onto each bowl. Garnish with the scallions and pepper; if you like, serve with your favorite hot sauce.

1 **poblano pepper**

1 **red bell pepper**

1 **green bell pepper**

8 ounces **Mexican chorizo**

2 tablespoons **olive oil**

1 small **onion**, thinly sliced

Kosher salt and freshly ground **black pepper**

2 **garlic cloves**, finely chopped

1 tablespoon **fresh lime juice**

2 tablespoons chopped **fresh cilantro**

4 large **eggs**

Classic Cheddar Grits (page 53), warmed

CHORIZO, PEPPER, AND ONION GRITS

Serves 4

These playful grits were inspired by an all-day neighborhood joint in New Orleans that has an ever-changing daily special of grits topped with, well, just about everything. The idea took hold at the Diner, where cheddar grits are a mainstay of the menu. We rotate the toppings frequently, but these and the Tomato, Chickpea, and Feta Grits (page 58) are two favorites—this one meaty and hefty and the other vegetarian and fairly light.

As the ingredients for each topping combination come together fairly quickly, make sure you have your grits (a full batch per the recipe on page 53) in their final low-and-slow stage of cooking before you begin.

Much of our back-of-the-house staff hails from the state of Puebla, in Mexico, and their influence is threaded through our menu. They inspire us to keep our food big on flavor, often with a liberal use of fresh and dried chiles. Here, roasted poblano and Mexican chorizo play off one another, building smoky layers of heat. This particular combination, which we use to top the grits (though you could certainly serve it over rice or baked polenta, if you prefer), is bold and warming. The addition of lime juice at the end helps cut the fat of the chorizo while also brightening everything up. It's an addictive combination.

1. Preheat the oven to 400°F and line a baking sheet with parchment paper.

2. Place the poblano and the red and green bell peppers on the baking sheet and roast for about 40 minutes, turning them once halfway through (you want the peppers to be soft, a bit deflated, and slightly charred). When they're done, remove them from the oven and set aside to cool.

3. Turn the oven down to 375°F. Put the chorizo in a small roasting pan or sauté pan and slide into the oven.

Roast the chorizo until it is browned on top and cooked through, 10 to 12 minutes.

4. While the chorizo is cooking, use the tip of a sharp paring knife to help you remove the pepper skins. Cut the peppers in half, use your fingers to pull out the seeds, and slice the peppers into thin strips.

5. When the chorizo is done, remove it from the oven. Drain any excess fat from the pan. Use a wooden spoon to crumble the chorizo, then set aside.

6. Heat the olive oil in a medium sauté pan over high heat. Add the onion slices, stirring frequently until they start to brown around the edges, 4 to 5 minutes. Reduce the heat to medium, season the onion with salt and pepper, and add the garlic. Cook until the onion is a deep caramel color and soft, another 2 to 3 minutes.

7. Add the chorizo and roasted peppers to the pan and toss to mix well. Add the lime juice and cilantro, stir, then taste for seasoning. Turn the heat to the lowest setting to keep the mixture warm while you poach your eggs (see page 29).

8. Divide the grits among 4 soup bowls. Top with the chorizo and pepper mixture, followed by a poached egg, then finish each serving with a pinch of salt and a sprinkle of freshly ground pepper atop the egg.

TOMATO, CHICKPEA, AND FETA GRITS

Serves 4

2 pints small **tomatoes** (such as grape, cherry, or sweet 100s), halved

¼ cup plus 2 tablespoons **olive oil**

1 sprig of **fresh thyme**

1 **garlic clove**

Kosher salt and freshly ground **black pepper**

2 cups cooked **chickpeas** (from 1 cup dried, liquid reserved), or one 16-ounce can, rinsed and drained (see Note)

2 tablespoons **fresh lemon juice**

1 teaspoon **paprika**

2 tablespoons chopped **fresh parsley**

4 large **eggs**

Classic Cheddar Grits (page 53), warmed

½ cup crumbled **feta cheese**

This combination is light enough to feel virtuous and sophisticated enough to impress. Oven-roasted tomatoes make for little red flavor bombs; chickpeas make for a creamy, almost meaty heft; and the sharp tang of fresh feta and a bit of fresh lemon juice snap everything to attention.

We've kept salting to a minimum here, but depending on whether you're using dried or canned chickpeas, and how salty your feta is, you may want more. As with all savory dishes, we recommend you taste along the way and adjust the seasoning to your liking.

1. Preheat the oven to 375°F and line a baking sheet with aluminum foil.

2. Put the tomatoes in a large mixing bowl and add 2 tablespoons of the olive oil, the thyme, and the garlic. Season the tomatoes lightly with salt and pepper and toss to mix thoroughly.

3. Spread the tomatoes on the baking sheet, cut side down, in a single layer, then slide the baking sheet into the oven and roast until the tomato skins begin to darken and blister, 20 to 25 minutes. Use a rubber spatula to turn the tomatoes over and cook for an additional 10 to 12 minutes, until the skins turn crispy and the flesh begins to dry out. Remove from the oven to cool.

4. Place the chickpeas into a medium saucepan along with ½ cup of water (or cooking liquid from the beans, or stock if you're substituting), the remaining ¼ cup of olive oil, the lemon juice, and the paprika. Over medium heat, bring the mixture just to a simmer, then add the roasted tomatoes and the parsley and stir. Turn the heat to the lowest setting to keep the mixture warm while you poach your eggs (per instructions on page 29).

5. Divide the grits among 4 soup bowls. Top each with some chickpea mixture and then with a poached egg. Sprinkle the feta evenly across the bowls, and finish each with a final pinch of salt and a sprinkle of fresh-cracked pepper.

NOTE: If you're using dried chickpeas, you'll want to soak them in double their volume of water (i.e., if you're making 1 cup dried chickpeas, soak them in 2 cups of water). Soak at least 8 hours, or overnight, at room temperature. When you're ready to cook, dump the whole thing—chickpeas and soaking water—into a large pot, bring to a boil, then lower to a simmer and cook until fork-tender, salting to taste only after they're fully cooked, but still warm. It's a good idea to cook more chickpeas than you need, as leftovers freeze beautifully in their cooking liquid, and keep virtually interminably in the freezer.

If you're using canned chickpeas rather than cooking your own from scratch, substitute water for the cooking liquid or, better yet, vegetable stock. Have your grits ready and warm before you begin assembling the chickpea topping.

CLASSIC BUTTERMILK PANCAKES

Serves 4; makes 14 to 16 pancakes

This recipe makes incredibly cakey, light pancakes with a buttermilk flavor; they're the familiar crowd-pleasing counterpart to our slightly moodier, darker Buckwheat Pancakes (page 65). Stack them high and serve them with whatever you like—butter, maple syrup, and/or a sprinkling of fresh berries.

A common mistake when cooking pancakes is to use too high a heat. Remember, pancakes are cakes, and like cakes you cook in the oven, they need moderate heat to cook evenly. Heating over high heat to try to speed up the process, then turning it back down, can lead to uneven heat (hot spots) in your pan.

Always make a test pancake. When your pan is hot and greased, pour in a small test pancake. The batter should spread evenly across the griddle or pan and then stop. If it is too thick, it will sit in a lump. To fix a thick batter, add liquid in very small increments: you don't want to thin the batter too much, as that will cause it to lose its ability to hold together. If you over-thin your batter and it begins dribbling uncontrollably toward the pan's edges as you pour it in, there's no turning back.

2¾ cups **all-purpose flour**

¼ cup **sugar**

½ teaspoon **salt**

1 tablespoon **baking powder**

½ teaspoon **baking soda**

2 large **eggs**

2½ cups **buttermilk**

½ teaspoon **vanilla extract**

1 cup (2 sticks) **unsalted butter**, melted

2 tablespoons **vegetable oil**

Softened butter and **maple syrup**, for serving

1. Sift the flour, sugar, salt, baking powder, and baking soda into a large bowl.

2. In a medium bowl, combine the eggs, buttermilk, and vanilla and whisk until smooth. Add the melted butter and whisk again to incorporate.

3. Set a griddle or cast-iron skillet over medium heat, giving it several minutes to warm evenly.

4. While the pan is getting hot, add 3 cups of the liquid mixture to the dry ingredients and gently fold together with a rubber spatula until well incorporated; a few small lumps are okay.

5. Brush the griddle with a bit of the vegetable oil. Make a small test pancake (see headnote). Once you've got your consistency right, drop the batter onto the griddle using a ¼ cup measure and repeat, leaving at least ½ inch between pancakes. Once the edges begin to brown and the bubbles stop coming through the top, about 2 minutes, turn the pancakes over and cook for an additional 2 to 3 minutes.

6. Serve immediately with the butter and maple syrup or keep the pancakes on a plate covered with a dry kitchen towel in a low oven (about 200°F) until all the batter is used up or until everyone is full.

A Grain by Any Other Name: Buckwheat

Surprising to many, buckwheat isn't a grain. Rather, it's the seed of a plant that is a relative of sorrel and rhubarb. Buckwheat grows quickly, which means it thrives in areas with short growing seasons (read: upper New York State), and has long been prized for its double use as both food and fertilizer. Buckwheat naturally fixes nitrogen, an essential nutrient, into soil, and so was long grown as a cover crop to help restore fertility to the soil. It can be prepared in a multitude of ways, including cooked as groats (commonly known as kasha) or ground into flour and used in baked goods and noodles (notably Japanese soba). It's an added bonus that buckwheat is exceptionally good for you and, for those who pay attention to such things, free of gluten.

The Hudson Valley and the Catskills were once the breadbasket of the Northeast, and buckwheat was frequently planted as a restorative cover crop. During the twentieth century, though, as nitrogen-based fertilizers began to replace crop rotation as a means of maintaining productivity in soil, buckwheat fell out of favor in American agriculture, and thus in American cooking. Grain growing, more generally, became more mechanized and was concentrated in the Midwest. Lucky for us, recent years have seen a revival of grain-growing in our region, which has brought buckwheat back into circulation. Sites like the Hudson Valley Farm Hub in Hurley, New York, are experimenting with both heritage and hybrid grains to learn which do best in our regional soils with today's climate. Many family farms have begun to grow and mill their own grains once again, making for exciting possibilities in the kitchen.

BUCKWHEAT PANCAKES

Serves 4; makes 14 to 16 pancakes

We feature both Classic Buttermilk Pancakes (page 63) as well as these buckwheat cakes, which are a bit denser and distinct in flavor, with a nutty, rich depth from using buckwheat flour.

These pancakes turn a dark brown. Don't worry, they're not burned; that's just the buckwheat talking. Serve them hot with your choice of toppings; ours come with sweet butter and plenty of local maple syrup, but yogurt, honey, fresh fruit, and preserves work nicely here as well.

1. Sift together the flours, sugar, salt, baking powder, and baking soda in a large mixing bowl.

2. In a medium mixing bowl, whisk together the eggs and buttermilk until smooth. Add the melted butter, then whisk again to incorporate thoroughly.

3. Set a griddle or cast-iron skillet over medium heat, giving it several minutes to warm evenly. Add the wet ingredients to the dry ingredients, and fold together gently just until the white flecks of flour have disappeared into the batter, being careful not to overmix (some small leftover lumps are okay).

4. Test your pan's heat: you're ready to cook when a flick of water onto the hot surface sizzles on contact. Brush the pan with some of the vegetable oil (a paper towel dipped into the oil works in lieu of a brush). Make a test pancake (see headnote, page 63) to check the consistency of your batter.

5. Working in batches, drop the batter in ¼ cup portions into the pan; repeat, leaving at least ½ inch between the pancakes. Once the edges begin to brown and the bubbles stop coming through the top, about 2 minutes, flip the pancakes and cook until the underside has taken on the same brown hue as what's now the top, 2 to 3 more minutes.

6. Serve immediately with butter and maple syrup, or keep the pancakes on a plate covered with a dry kitchen towel in a low oven (about 200ºF) until all the batter is used up or until everyone is full.

1 cup **all-purpose flour**

2 cups **buckwheat flour**

¼ cup **sugar**

1 teaspoon **kosher salt**

1 teaspoon **baking powder**

½ teaspoon **baking soda**

2 large **eggs**

4 cups **buttermilk**

6 tablespoons **unsalted butter**, melted

2 tablespoons **vegetable oil**

Softened butter and **maple syrup**, for serving

SPICY TURKEY SAUSAGE

Serves 4

2 teaspoons **kosher salt**

1 teaspoon grated **fresh ginger** (about a 1½-inch knob)

1 large **garlic clove**, grated

1 teaspoon **ground sage**

1 teaspoon freshly ground **black pepper**

1 tablespoon **maple syrup**

½ teaspoon **red pepper flakes**

1 pound **ground turkey** (see Note)

2 tablespoons **ice water**

2 tablespoons **vegetable** or **canola oil**, or other high-heat cooking oil

This is a fresh patty sausage, light on fat (thanks, turkey!) and big on flavor. We use classic seasonings: sage and maple, with a good kick of heat from fresh ginger, garlic, red pepper flakes, and black pepper. This is a great recipe for those intimidated by sausage-making paraphernalia—there's no casing involved, no tying of links, no aging needed. It's incredibly simple and fast to bring together.

....

1. In a large bowl, stir together the salt, ginger, garlic, sage, pepper, maple syrup, and red pepper flakes. Add the turkey and, using your hands, squish everything together repeatedly. It will start to transform from clumpy to tacky, smooth, and uniformly consistent. Drizzle the water over the mixture and keep squishing until the water is fully incorporated.

2. Working with slightly damp hands, divide the meat into 4 equal portions, rolling each into a ball between your hands. Place the balls on a plate or small baking sheet and chill for at least 30 minutes.

3. When you're about ready to eat, heat a large heavy skillet over medium-high heat. When a droplet of water dropped into the skillet sizzles and quickly disappears, you're ready to cook. Pour the vegetable oil into the pan. Then take a sausage ball and lay it toward one edge of the pan. With a metal spatula, press down until you form a patty about ½ inch thick. Working quickly, repeat with the other 3 sausage balls. Cook the patties, undisturbed, so they form a brown crust, about 4 minutes, then flip, cooking until the other side is browned and crusty, 4 minutes more. To check for doneness, cut into the center of one patty—there should be no pink left in the center, but the patties will still be very moist. Remove from the pan and serve immediately.

NOTE: You want your turkey extremely cold, so keep it in the fridge until you're ready to add it to the seasoning mixture. This way, rather than melting, the turkey fat emulsifies into the meat-and-spice mixture.

This sausage can be made up to 3 days ahead and cooked when you're ready to eat.

CRISPY BELGIAN WAFFLES

Serves 6; makes six 6-inch waffles

1¾ cups **all-purpose flour**

¼ cup **sugar**

1 teaspoon **kosher salt**

1 tablespoon **baking powder**

4 large **eggs**, separated

1½ cups **whole milk**

½ cup (1 stick) **unsalted butter**, melted and slightly cooled

Cooking spray or **vegetable oil** (such as grapeseed)

Softened butter, maple syrup, fruit, and/or whipped cream, for serving

Waffles. Classic. Done well, there's little that's more satisfying. When we first opened, we had a single household waffle maker. It lasted two weeks of pumping out forty orders per day. We learned our lesson and rapidly upgraded to a commercial unit. We still have to replace it every four months, though.

Waffle batter is similar to pancake batter, but with more butter. Some recipes, like ours, also make use of whipped egg whites for a lightening effect. At the Diner, we use Belgian waffle irons. Belgian waffles are thick and have deep crevices, which leads to more crispy edges.

Make these as a breakfast treat, or serve them for dessert. The recipe doubles nicely if you're feeding a crowd.

1. Preheat a Belgian waffle iron to medium heat.

2. Into a large bowl, sift together the flour, sugar, salt, and baking powder. In a medium bowl, combine the egg yolks and milk and whisk together. Add the melted butter and whisk to incorporate. Add the egg yolk mixture to the flour mixture and gently mix with a rubber spatula until smooth.

3. Place the egg whites in another medium bowl. Use a whisk or hand mixer to whip the egg whites until they double in volume and hold stiff peaks (you're looking to be able to spike them like Sonic the Hedgehog's hair) when the whisk is lifted. (You can also use a stand mixer if you have one.) Add one-third of the whipped egg whites to the rest of the batter and use a rubber spatula to

gently fold them in. Continue adding the egg whites in thirds until fully incorporated.

4. Spray the preheated waffle iron with cooking spray or use a pastry brush or paper towel to lightly coat it with oil. Add enough of the batter to fill the iron to within ½ inch of the edge (about 1 cup of batter for a 6-inch waffle iron). Cook to the specifications of your waffle iron (watching for the steaming to slow before checking for doneness) until golden brown and delicious. Keep the waffles warm on a baking sheet in a 200°F oven while you finish cooking off the batter.

5. Serve immediately with butter, maple syrup, fruit, and whipped cream, or whatever else you fancy.

BRIOCHE FRENCH TOAST

Serves 4

Are you one of the many people who never order French toast at a diner because it's bound to be limp, thin, and uninspiring? Making French toast from pre-sliced sandwich bread is just sad, and if that's all the French toast you've ever experienced, you've got no idea what you're missing. Served in thick slabs, this French toast is fortifyingly rich, sweet, and eggy.

Buy the best brioche you can find for this recipe (or, if you're an experienced or adventurous home baker, try your hand at making your own). Just remember: the bread matters. A lot.

1 loaf **brioche**

5 large **eggs**

1 cup **heavy cream**

1 cup **whole milk**

½ cup **orange juice**

½ cup **sugar**

2 teaspoons **ground cinnamon**

Pinch of **ground nutmeg**

4 tablespoons (½ stick) **unsalted butter**

Maple syrup, warmed for serving

1. Cut off the ends of the brioche and slice the remaining loaf into eight 1½-inch-thick slices. Cut each slice diagonally to create 16 triangles. Leave the sliced bread out for a few hours (or overnight in a paper bag or bread box) so that it dries out slightly; this will help it soak up more of the eggy mixture.

2. In a medium bowl, whisk together the eggs, cream, milk, orange juice, sugar, cinnamon, and nutmeg. Pour the mixture into a large baking dish. Lay 4 brioche triangles into the egg mixture and then, starting with the one you placed first, turn each one over to fully coat the bread.

3. Heat a large skillet over medium-high heat. Add 1 tablespoon of butter to the pan. Once it melts and begins to bubble slightly, carefully use your fingers to transfer each brioche slice to the pan. Cook until it turns golden brown and crispy, 2 to 3 minutes. Flip and cook the other side for 2 to 3 more minutes. Then stand the slices on their long, diagonally sliced edge; the crusted points of the toast triangles will be pointed straight into the air here. Cook until golden brown, 2 to 3 minutes. Repeat until all of the bread slices are cooked. (If you're not working a short-order breakfast, you can keep the toast warm on a baking sheet in a 200°F oven.) Serve with warm maple syrup.

ARNOLD BENNETT SKILLET
(A.K.A. SOFT SCRAMBLED EGGS WITH SMOKED TROUT)

Serves 4

8 large **eggs**

4 tablespoons (½ stick) **unsalted butter**

1 cup **flaked smoked trout** (about 4 whole fillets), in small pieces

1 cup grated **parmesan cheese**

8 tablespoons (½ cup) **crème fraîche**

4 tablespoons finely chopped **fresh chives**

If there's one Phoenicia Diner dish that signals to guests that they're not in an old-school diner, it's this. From day one, this beguiling skillet dish has been a touchstone of our menu, something like our mission statement on a plate: classic Americana with a boost of sophistication, a hint of whimsy, and a deep sense of place.

Arnold Bennett (1867–1931) was a British novelist and critic whose optimistic take on things—people, the world, and smoked fish, he believed, were generally good—set him at odds with the fusty Bloomsbury set. While penning one of his novels, he settled in at the Savoy hotel in London, where an eponymous omelet was developed to his liking. His was enriched with smoked haddock and hollandaise. At the Phoenicia Diner, local trout is swapped in for the haddock, and crème fraîche for hollandaise. The result is a creamy, luscious scramble, studded with salty smoked trout and given a hint of tang and body from the crème fraîche.

1. Break the eggs into a medium bowl and beat with a whisk until fully combined.

2. Melt the butter in a heavy skillet over medium-high heat. Once it starts to bubble rapidly and turn brown, add the smoked trout. Cook for 1 minute, just to warm through.

3. Add the eggs to the pan and stir gently with a wooden spoon or rubber spatula to prevent the eggs from burning (see Note). When the eggs are almost set but still runny (this will take a couple of minutes at most), remove the skillet from the heat and add the parmesan and crème fraîche, stirring briefly to incorporate. Top with the chives, and serve immediately.

NOTE: You need to work quickly so your eggs don't stick and you can incorporate the other ingredients, so make sure you have all your ingredients prepped and beside you at the stove when you begin cooking. The residual heat from the skillet will finish cooking the eggs, so don't worry that we ask you to pull them off the heat when they're still runny.

The Roots of Folk Music in the Catskills

Before Janis and Jimi went to Woodstock, there was Pete—Pete Seeger, that is—and Camp Woodland.

In 1930, a group of idealists purchased an old church and its surrounding land just outside Phoenicia, New York. As the nation industrialized, they saw, too, the growing divide along lines of race, class, and religion. Away from the pressures of New York City, this small group of egalitarians aimed to create a place where a diverse group of people could come to learn, and help to preserve, traditional rural ways of life. The ringleaders, helmed by educator and director Norman Studer, would invite young folks from many walks of life and send them out into the community to gather stories, lessons, and songs, thus inoculating them at an early age with the values of neighborliness and respect. Studer and his colleagues welcomed their first campers in 1939, and they called the place Camp Woodland.

Studer was a sight to behold, bumping along country roads in his wood-sided Ford station wagon (similar to the one featured in the Diner's logo), campers packed in like sardines. The campers were tasked with asking around for the keepers of the region's folkways, then were driven around to find them. One such cultural gem was

George Edwards, who lived in a rented room at a nearby farm, his concave chest revealing the damage done by a lumbering accident long ago. Holding court beside a hulking cookstove, he pulled folk songs from memory—many of them Irish, English, and Scottish, like the people who worked the region's industries. While he sang, campers and Herbert Haufrecht, the camp's musicologist, scribbled notes. For a decade, Edwards was a mainstay at Camp Woodland, living part of every summer at the campground, singing for campers and offering up his knowledge for the record.

While the camp's mission wasn't explicitly musical—craftsmanship, foodways, and local lore were also sources of interest to the Woodlanders— folk music became central to Woodland's culture; the camp became known for its nightly performances and weekly square dances, fostering a sort of utopian cultural exchange between locals, campers, and counselors.

In 1948, Camp Woodland held its second annual Folk Festival of the Catskills. Pete Seeger— then twenty-nine years old—had begun visiting the camp a couple of years before, and had found a sympathetic community among the Woodlanders. Seeger, a prolific songwriter in his own right, was also a prodigious collector of old folk tunes, and Woodland offered him a chance to perform, teach, and learn. In 1948, Seeger was asked to perform on the heels of George Edwards. As he strode onstage with his banjo, he said, "I only wish and hope that when I am eighty-odd years old I can remember as many songs as George Edwards can."

Camp Woodland was unabashedly political. As the lingering effects of the Depression settled over the land, more and more thinkers and educators sought to divorce themselves from what they saw as the cruel and ultimately doomed forces of capitalism. Paying attention to traditional ways of life, and the elders who'd both endured and sustained it, represented a radical rejection of the American obsession with newness, money, and technology. In the early 1950s, as Seeger's outspoken politics gained attention, he struggled to find work. Studer offered him a job as music director at the Downtown Community School in lower Manhattan. In 1955, Seeger was subpoenaed to testify before the House Un-American Activities Committee. Refusing to speak, citing the First Amendment, by March of 1961 he was indicted for contempt of Congress and convicted.

Meanwhile, Camp Woodland was preparing for a folk concert at New York City's Town Hall on April 5, 1961. The theme was to be Upstate Meets Downstate. At the last minute, the Appeals Court granted Seeger bail pending appeal the day before the concert, and he walked onstage to be greeted by a packed house and uproarious cheers. Just over a year later, Seeger's conviction was overturned.

Seeger went on to become America's most famous folk singer, with a seemingly never-ending supply of tunes in his repertoire. He continued to visit Camp Woodland until its demise in 1962, believing until his death, in 2014, that traditional ways of life held an important place in American culture, and singing about the values of acceptance, peace, and neighborliness so personified by Camp Woodland.

While Camp Woodland was shuttered in the early '60s, folk music had, by then, firmly taken root in the Catskills. Manhattan-based entertainment manager Albert "The Baron of Bearsville" Grossman brought the likes of Van Morrison, Jimi Hendrix, The Band, and Joan Baez to perform at his home. Bob Dylan, in a fit of paranoia, moved his family to the town of Woodstock. There, in a house called "Big Pink," he wrote some of his most famous songs. Dylan brought to town Levon Helm, whose studio still hosts a dazzling lineup of intimate shows in Woodstock. Most famously, in 1969, the Woodstock music festival (which borrowed its name from the town but took place in Bethel, in neighboring Sullivan County) made the Catskills synonymous with free love, music, and a joy-filled rejection of the status quo.

These hills are still alive with the sound of music. Steve Earle has taken up the mantle of Studer, Seeger, and their peers at Camp Woodland, holding a songwriting camp in Big Indian each summer. Bethel Woods still puts on major shows every summer season, and Bob Dylan recently came back to play the Hutton Brickyards in Kingston. Top-of-the-line recording studios are tucked away on either side of the Hudson River, and the whole region is studded with music venues, with more arriving every year. Places like the Colony and Bearsville Theater in Woodstock, BSP and the Ulster County Performing Arts Center in Kingston, and The Falcon in Marlboro command top billings. Due to the area's resurgence, even our local bars can now book world-class acts; sitting at the Catskills Pines in Mount Tremper or The Beverly in Kingston, watching a live performance of the sort most have to drive to a big city to hear, it feels like you're in on a glorious secret.

In this region of woodlands and farms, the proliferation and growth of the music community still seems something of an anomaly. But now as before, the place fosters alternatives to convention and complacency, shelters the free-thinking among us, and invites us to reimagine a better future without forgetting the past that still echoes all around us.

2 tablespoons **vegetable oil**

1 large **onion**, diced

Kosher salt and freshly ground **black pepper**

1 pound **smoked ham**, cut into ½-inch cubes

Phoenician Potatoes with Rosemary Salt (page 42)

6 ounces **sharp white cheddar cheese**, grated (about 1½ cups)

4 large **eggs**

INTERSTATE 77 REVISITED
(A.K.A. CHEESE- AND HAM-SMOTHERED HASH BROWNS)

Serves 4

For Chef Chris, Interstate 77, which passes through the North Carolina town where he grew up, has none of the romance of Woodstock hero Bob Dylan's "Highway 61" nor the sweeping scenery of the Diner's Route 28, but it does carry its own nostalgia: high school nights spent speeding along the backroads for fun before, inevitably, ending up at the Waffle House. In the South, no matter where you might find yourself, you never need to travel more than an exit or two before spotting that familiar yellow-blocked sign rising over an exit ramp, promising hot coffee and greasy, satisfying grub. Chris's late-night go-to was cheese- and ham-smothered hash browns. This is a (slightly) more grown-up rendition, though it promises all the satisfaction of the version he craved back then. At Waffle House, the piped-in music would've been George Strait, Hank Williams Jr., or Garth Brooks, but given the Diner's home here in the Catskills, it seemed only appropriate to tip our hats to Mr. Dylan in this dish's title.

1. Preheat the oven to 350°F. Heat a 12-inch cast-iron skillet over medium-high heat.

2. Pour the vegetable oil into the skillet and wait until it just begins to smoke. Add the onion and sauté until golden brown, stirring occasionally to avoid burning, 7 to 8 minutes. Lightly season the onion with salt and pepper.

3. Add the ham and potatoes to the pan and toss to mix. Remove the pan from the heat and top the potatoes and ham evenly with the cheddar cheese. Slide the pan into the oven, cooking just long enough to melt the cheese, about 5 minutes.

4. Cook the eggs sunny-side up (see page 29), then slide them on top of the cheesy ham and potato skillet. Serve immediately.

TRUE GREENS AND GRITS

Serves 4

2 bunches **collard greens**

2 tablespoons **vegetable oil**

4 ounces thick-sliced **bacon**, diced

1 cup diced **onion**

4 **garlic cloves**, minced

Pinch of **red pepper flakes**

1 cup strong brewed **coffee**

½ cup **apple cider vinegar**

4 cups **chicken stock**

Kosher salt and freshly ground **black pepper**

Classic Cheddar Grits (page 53), kept warm

8 large **eggs**

Hot sauce, for serving (optional)

For Chef Chris, in his native North Carolina, a side of bitter greens graces most meals. They're an acquired taste, though, and even some native-born Southerners don't care for them (his mom, Joy, included). But she has taken to these, which have little in common with the limp steam-table greens so ubiquitous in the South. These are robust and fortifying, with plenty of bracing flavor from the cider vinegar, garlic, red pepper flakes, and even coffee (a bitterness-enhancing tip borrowed from red eye gravy). Any cooking greens will thrive in this mixture, but collards have more structural integrity than leafier ones. Served simply over grits with an egg, this combination makes for a deeply warming and healthy meal.

Start the greens and get them to the low-and-slow stage of cooking before you start cooking the pre-soaked grits. Alternatively, make the greens the night before, when you set your grits to soak; all you'll have left to do when you're getting ready to eat is cook your grits and the eggs.

. . . .

1. Rinse the collard greens under running water to remove any grit. Cut off the tough bottom portions of the stems. Using the tip of a knife, cut the leaves down the middle lengthwise, then roll the leaves up, lengthwise, into a tight cigar shape and cut them into half-inch strips.

2. Heat a Dutch oven (or other heavy-bottomed pot with a lid) over medium-high heat, then add the vegetable oil and bacon. Cook, stirring frequently, until the bacon is browned and crispy, 4 to 5 minutes. Next into the pot go the onion and garlic. Cook until the onion begins to turn translucent, about another 5 minutes. Sprinkle in the red pepper flakes.

3. Pile the collard greens into the pot and stir to mix everything. Reduce the heat to medium, cover, and cook until the greens are wilted and bright green, 10 to 12 minutes.

4. Pour in the coffee and vinegar, and cover again to steam the greens for 5 minutes. Pour in the chicken stock, sprinkle in 2 teaspoons salt and 1 teaspoon pepper, and reduce the heat to medium-low so the potlikker is at a low simmer. Cover the pot again and continue to cook until the greens are very soft and have turned the color of dark camouflage, about 2 hours.

5. If you haven't already done so, this is the time to cook your grits (see page 53).

6. When the grits and greens are both ready, divide the warm grits among 4 bowls and top each serving with collard greens. Cook the eggs sunny-side up (see page 29), then slide 2 eggs onto each bowl. Finish with a pinch of salt and pepper, as well as some hot sauce, if you like.

FORAGER'S SKILLET
WITH RAMPS AND PORK BELLY

Serves 4

8 whole **ramps**
(bulbs and leaves)

1 tablespoon
vegetable oil

Cured Pork Belly
(recipe follows), cut
into ½-inch cubes

**Phoenician Potatoes
with Rosemary Salt**
(page 42)

Kosher salt and
freshly ground
black pepper

4 large **eggs**

Ramps, a member of the allium family like leeks, garlic, and onions, are one of the first signs of spring to emerge in mountain regions. They bring with them the promise of warmer weather and tremendous excitement for those who love to cook and eat. Around the Catskills, ramps are a carefully guarded resource. As with a secret trout pool or "honey hole," the locals are happy to share their bounty, but not their source's location. If you do manage to squeeze some intel out of a local forager, it's usually vague and suspect, like "at the rock that looks like a bear, make a left."

Giddiness about ramp season is often tempered by sticker shock at the farmers or specialty markets. So, imagine our delight when Kenny, a longtime friend of the Diner, came in and offered us an armful of ramps from his property—for free. A glut of any product stirs creativity, and this recipe was the result of Kenny's generous gift. Here, we use ramps to offset the richness of the pork belly. This makes for a decadent, impressive skillet—one that flies out of the kitchen each time we offer it as a special.

If ramps are out of season, or you can't find them at your local farmers market, you can substitute 8 scallions and 4 cloves of garlic; the flavor won't be exactly the same, but you'll get the necessary green allium kick.

Plan ahead here. You'll need time (ideally overnight) to prepare and cure the pork belly, and you'll want to have your potatoes prepared before you begin assembling the skillet itself.

1. Preheat the oven to 300°F.

2. Separate the leaves of the ramps from the bulbs and stems. Cut the bulbs and stems into ¼-inch rounds, and cut the greens crosswise into ¼-inch strips.

3. Heat a large ovenproof skillet, like cast-iron, over high heat. Pour the vegetable oil into the pan and add the pork belly. Cook, stirring the pork occasionally, until it is evenly brown and crispy on all sides, 4 or 5 minutes. Add the ramp stems and bulbs and continue to cook, without stirring, until the leaves are wilted and the bulbs have become slightly translucent, about 2 more minutes.

4. Add the potatoes and ramp greens, and stir to combine, then remove from the heat. Season to taste with salt and pepper. Slide the skillet into the oven just to heat the skillet through, 4 to 5 minutes.

5. Meanwhile, cook the eggs sunny-side up (see page 29). Pull the skillet from the oven, top with the eggs, and serve immediately.

Cured Pork Belly

Makes about 1½ pounds

2 pounds fresh **pork belly**, skin removed

¼ cup **kosher salt**

¼ cup packed **dark brown sugar**

1 **garlic clove**, finely minced

1 teaspoon **Spanish paprika**

½ teaspoon **ground ginger**

½ teaspoon **ground fennel seed**

½ teaspoon **freshly ground black pepper**

½ teaspoon **cayenne pepper**

1. Place the pork belly in a large glass or ceramic baking dish. Mix the salt, brown sugar, garlic, and spices in a medium bowl, then sprinkle the spice mixture generously over the meat and massage it into the flesh to coat evenly. Cover with plastic and leave in the refrigerator overnight or up to 24 hours.

2. The next day, position an oven rack at the lowest setting and preheat the oven to 350°F. Remove the pork from the fridge and pat dry with a towel, leaving on the rub that's clung to the meat, but scraping off any extra spice rub that has pooled at the base of the meat. Cook the meat for 30 minutes. Carefully pour the rendered fat from the dish into a bowl or empty can and return the pork to the oven to roast until the meat is dark brown and soft to the touch, about another 30 minutes. Remove the meat from the oven and pour off the rendered fat again.

3. Once the pork is cool to the touch, wrap in plastic and place in the fridge until it is fully chilled and firm, at least 2 hours and preferably overnight. (Keeps up to 2 weeks, wrapped tightly in plastic, in the refrigerator.)

ROASTED ROOTS AND EGGS
WITH PARSLEY PESTO
Serves 4

1 large **celery root**, peeled and cut into ½-inch cubes (2 cups)

1 medium **butternut squash**, peeled and cut into ½-inch cubes (2 cups)

4 to 6 **parsnips**, peeled and cut into ½-inch cubes (2 cups)

4 medium **carrots**, cut into ½-inch cubes (2 cups)

1 large **potato**, peeled and cut into ½-inch cubes (2 cups)

6 to 8 **sunchokes** (Jerusalem artichokes), scrubbed and trimmed of any mushy or rotten bits, cut into ½-inch cubes (2 cups)

¼ cup **olive oil**

¼ cup **fresh thyme leaves**

Kosher salt and freshly ground **black pepper**

4 large **eggs**

Parsley Pesto (recipe follows)

When winter is hard upon us and fresh vegetables are difficult to come by, we pull out this recipe. It makes use of all the summer bounty that has been put into cold storage for later use. Roasting the root vegetables highlights their natural sweetness and brings out a lovely richness, but contrast is needed to keep things from feeling too monotonous. Here, we brighten things up with a good drizzle of lemony parsley pesto.

We serve this with a fried egg at the Diner to make it a meal, but if you omit the egg, this makes a terrific side for roasted meats or fish.

1. Preheat the oven to 400°F. Line 2 baking sheets with parchment paper.

2. Place the celery root, squash, parsnips, carrots, potatoes, and sunchokes in a large mixing bowl. Add the olive oil and thyme, and season with salt and pepper. Toss all the vegetables to evenly coat with the oil and seasonings.

3. Spread the vegetables on the baking sheets, making sure they form only one layer. Roast for 20 minutes. Remove from the oven and use a metal spatula or kitchen spoon to flip the vegetables to ensure even cooking. Return to the oven and continue to cook until the vegetables are dark brown, even almost burnt in spots, and soft, 20 to 25 minutes more.

4. Divide the vegetables among 4 plates.

5. Cook the eggs sunny-side up (see page 29). Top each plate with an egg and drizzle liberally with the pesto. Serve immediately.

RECIPE CONTINUES ➤

Parsley Pesto

Makes 1 heaping cup

½ cup **walnuts**

2 cups roughly chopped **fresh flat-leaf parsley** (about 1 bunch)

1 teaspoon grated **lemon zest**

¾ cup **extra-virgin olive oil**, plus more as needed

¼ cup grated **parmesan cheese**

Kosher salt and freshly ground **black pepper**

1. Preheat the oven to 300°F.

2. Place the walnuts on a baking sheet and toast in the oven until brown and fragrant, 8 to 10 minutes. Remove from the oven and allow to cool completely.

3. Place the walnuts, parsley, lemon zest, and ¼ cup olive oil in a food processor. Pulse the processor a few times to form a thick coarse paste. Add the remaining ½ cup olive oil and the parmesan. Season with salt and pepper, then run the processor for 15 to 20 seconds, until the pesto is smooth and all the bits are finely chopped (this should be a loose pesto for drizzling on the veggies; add a bit more olive oil if needed to achieve the right consistency). (Keeps up to 3 days, tightly covered, in the refrigerator.)

CIDER-BRAISED DUCK AND GRITS
WITH BRUSSELS SPROUTS AND BUTTERNUT SQUASH

Serves 4

A lot of people love duck but are scared to cook it. Cider-braised duck is a great beginner's recipe (hard to mess up and so tasty) and a terrific preparation to add to your winter repertoire.

This dish, along with all our other skillets, is on the breakfast side of our menu at the Diner, but it makes an equally satisfying lunch or dinner. It's ideal cold-weather food—deeply comforting, but a bit elegant and complex, a treat for yourself or a guest.

Making the duck is a two-day process. If you like, you can braise the duck a day ahead—it keeps nicely. When you take it out of the refrigerator to reheat, you'll see a layer of fat on top. Just warm the duck in a saucepan over low heat, and the fat will reincorporate.

1. Preheat the oven to 400°F.

2. On a baking sheet, drizzle the Brussels sprouts and squash with the olive oil, season with salt and pepper, then spread in one even layer. Roast until the vegetables are browned and slightly crispy, 20 to 25 minutes. (If you've cooked the duck ahead of time, add the duck to the pan with the root vegetables for the last 2 to 3 minutes of roasting, just long enough to warm the meat through.)

3. When the vegetables are done cooking, transfer them to a large mixing bowl and add the duck. Toss everything together and keep warm.

4. Divide the warm grits among 4 serving bowls and top each bowl with the duck and vegetable mixture. Poach the eggs (see page 29) and place one egg on each serving, then sprinkle with parsley and a pinch of salt and pepper.

2 cups (8 ounces) **Brussels sprouts**, stems trimmed and any brown or yellow leaves removed

2 cups small-diced **butternut squash** (about half a medium squash)

2 tablespoons **olive oil**

Kosher salt and freshly ground **black pepper**

Cider-Braised Duck (recipe follows)

Classic Cheddar Grits (page 53), heated to piping hot

4 large **eggs**

2 tablespoons chopped **fresh parsley**

RECIPE CONTINUES ➼

Cider-Braised Duck

Makes about 2½ cups

2 tablespoons **kosher salt**

2 tablespoons loosely packed **dark brown sugar**

1 teaspoon freshly ground **black pepper**

2 **duck legs** (about 1 pound each)

1 quart **apple cider**

1 quart **chicken** or **duck stock**

1 small **onion**, thinly sliced

2 **garlic cloves**, smashed

2 sprigs of **fresh thyme**

1. In a large baking dish, add the salt, brown sugar, and pepper and mix thoroughly with your hands. Pat the duck legs dry with a clean towel and place them in the baking dish, sprinkling the sugar mixture liberally all over the duck legs. Cover with plastic wrap and refrigerate for at least 8 hours, or overnight.

2. The next day, preheat the oven to 300°F.

3. In a small Dutch oven or other heavy ovenproof pan, combine the duck legs, cider, stock, onion, garlic, and thyme. Bring just to a simmer over high heat, so small bubbles begin to form around the edges. Remove from the heat, cover the pot with a tight-fitting lid, and slide into the oven. Cook until the duck legs are very tender and you can easily pull the meat apart with a fork or your fingers, about 3 hours. Remove the pot from the oven and allow the duck to cool in its stock, uncovered.

4. Once the duck is cool to the touch, use your fingers to carefully remove the skin, bones, and connective tissue. Pull apart the meat, leaving it in large, bite-size pieces. (Once picked, the duck meat will keep up to 5 days, covered tightly, in the fridge.) Strain the liquid and reserve for other uses (makes a great base for a soup or can be frozen and used for another round of braised duck), save the bones for stock if you like, and discard the skin and connective tissue.

HOMEMADE CORNED BEEF HASH

Serves 4

On most diner menus, you'll find a corned beef hash. In theory, this is a terrific dish—little bits of long-brined meat crisped up in a pan with plenty of onions and some fresh bell peppers to cut through the fat. Unfortunately, most of the time, diner corned beef comes from a can, and as a result, a lot of folks don't think highly of the dish. This must be rectified. Real corned beef is incredibly flavorful and remarkably easy to make. Most of the flavor comes from a good long brining session—five days for ours—followed by low-and-slow cooking. There's no fuss, just incredibly succulent meat that makes for a hearty brunch.

At the Diner, we utilize most of our corned beef for this crowd-pleasing skillet, which stays on our menu year-round. But corned beef has many uses: slice the meat and make hot, open-faced sandwiches, chill and layer onto soft bread for a packed lunch, and by all means, pull out this recipe on St. Patrick's Day. Serve it simply and traditionally, alongside boiled cabbage and potatoes, or follow our lead and shred the meat into tortillas and top with shredded crunchy cabbage and a little hot sauce for a taco-style variation.

¼ cup **olive oil**

1 large **onion**, cut into ½-inch cubes (about 2 cups)

1 **green bell pepper**, cored, seeded, and cut into ½-inch pieces (about 1 cup)

1 **red bell pepper**, cored, seeded, and cut into ½-inch pieces (about 1 cup)

Corned Beef (recipe follows)

4 cups **Phoenician Potatoes with Rosemary Salt** (½ recipe; page 42)

4 large **eggs**

Kosher salt and freshly ground **black pepper**

1. Heat a large skillet over high heat and add the olive oil. Put the onion and bell peppers in the pan and cook, stirring occasionally, until they soften and begin to brown slightly, about 5 minutes.

2. Add the corned beef and stir once to mix well with the onion and peppers. Cook, stirring occasionally, until the meat begins to brown and stick to the pan slightly, another 5 to 6 minutes. Add a splash of water and stir with a wooden spoon to loosen the meat from the pan. Add the potatoes, stir to combine, and heat the potatoes through, 3 to 4 minutes.

3. Divide the corned beef and potatoes among 4 plates. Cook the eggs sunny-side up (see page 29) and top each plate with an egg. Season with salt and pepper, and serve immediately.

RECIPE CONTINUES ➤

Corned Beef

Makes 1¼ to 1½ pounds

2 cups **kosher salt**

1 cup packed **dark brown sugar**

3 tablespoons plus 1 teaspoon **pink curing salt**

7 **garlic cloves**

1 teaspoon **coriander seeds**

1 teaspoon **fennel seeds**

1 teaspoon **yellow mustard seeds**

1 teaspoon **black peppercorns**

1 teaspoon **whole cloves**

½ teaspoon **red pepper flakes**

5 sprigs of **fresh thyme**

3 dried **bay leaves**

2 pounds **beef brisket**, preferably the deckle (or fatty cut)

1 medium **onion**, roughly chopped

1 medium **carrot**, roughly chopped

2 **celery stalks**, roughly chopped

1. In a stockpot, combine the salt, brown sugar, pink salt, garlic, coriander seeds, fennel seeds, mustard seeds, peppercorns, cloves, red pepper flakes, thyme sprigs, and bay leaves with 1 gallon (16 cups) water. Bring to a boil over high heat, stirring to make sure the sugar dissolves and doesn't burn on the bottom, then cut the heat. Allow the liquid to cool to room temperature, then refrigerate until it is completely chilled, at least 2 hours.

2. Place the brisket in the brine and weight it down with a plate or bowl so that it remains completely submerged. Cover the pot and leave the brisket to cure in the fridge for 5 days, no more and no less.

3. Position the oven rack on the middle setting and preheat the oven to 225°F.

4. Remove the brisket from the brine and pick off any spices or herbs that are clinging to the meat. Place the brisket in a large Dutch oven or other heavy lidded pot. Cover the brisket with fresh water and add the onion, carrot, and celery. Bring the liquid to a boil over high heat, then remove from the heat. Cover the pot and place it in the oven. Cook the brisket, covered, until it is easy to pierce with a fork, yields slightly to the touch, and has a pink hue, about 3 hours. Remove the pot from the oven, uncover, and allow the brisket to cool to room temperature. Remove the brisket from the pot and refrigerate, uncovered, until completely cool, at least 3 hours or overnight. Discard the brining liquid, spices, and vegetables.

5. Once the brisket is cool, trim away any excess surface fat and dice the meat into 1-inch cubes. Store in the fridge in an airtight container for up to 2 weeks.

SOUPS, SALADS, AND SANDWICHES

CHICKEN TORTILLA SOUP

Serves 6 to 8

A hearty, warming chicken-based soup is requisite at any American diner. The specific *kind* of chicken soup, though, can tell you a lot about who owns the place or who's working in the kitchen—chicken and wild rice soup is common near the Great Lakes, matzoh ball soup is in the delis and diners of the Lower East Side and Jewish neighborhoods of Brooklyn, avoglemono is at your classic Greek diner, and good old American chicken noodle soup is, well, just about anywhere. At the Phoenicia Diner, our kitchen is staffed with a dedicated crew, many of whose roots are in Mexico, so you see their influences on our menu. This tortilla soup has been on the menu since day one, and it quickly became a favorite. Come chilly fall weather and then ski season, we can hardly make the stuff fast enough. It's rich in body, with a touch of heat from homemade chile paste that's offset with plenty of sliced avocado, and topped with crunchy tortilla strips. This soup is delicate in flavor but substantial enough to make a meal of.

The recipe calls for a number of common Mexican ingredients—varieties of chiles, Mexican oregano, and fresh epazote. All of these are usually available at Latin markets, but if you're struggling to find them, the internet offers a plethora of sourcing options these days. If you can't find fresh epazote, which has a pungent, slightly medicinal flavor, substitute tarragon and/or mint; the flavor will, indeed, be different but still delicious. Mexican oregano (which is citrusy and is actually a member of the lavender family) is preferable here. However, Mediterranean (or Greek) oregano, a member of the mint family, is more commonly found in American markets, and it will do if that's all you can get your hands on.

1. Place the chicken in a large stockpot and cover with 2 gallons (32 cups) of water. Bring the water up to a boil and reduce the heat to low, so the liquid is just barely bubbling. Cook, uncovered, until the chicken is tender and you can easily pull it apart with a fork, about 1 hour. Remove the chicken from the pot and set aside to cool, leaving the broth in the pot.

2. While the chicken is cooking, heat 2 to 3 inches of vegetable oil in a deep pot or Dutch oven to 375°F. Line a bowl with paper towels. Drop the tortilla strips in, a handful at a time, and fry until golden brown, about 1 minute. Using a slotted spoon, transfer the strips to the paper towel–lined bowl and season with salt. Repeat until all the strips are fried.

1 whole **chicken** (3 to 4 pounds)

Vegetable oil, for frying

10 **corn tortillas**, cut into ½-inch strips

Kosher salt

2 large **yellow onions**, cut into large chunks

5 medium **carrots**, cut into chunks

5 **celery stalks**, cut into thick slices

2 cups **Red Chile Paste** (recipe follows; see Note)

3 sprigs of **fresh epazote**, finely chopped (including stems)

Freshly ground **black pepper**

2 ripe **avocados**, sliced or cut into chunks

½ bunch **fresh cilantro**, finely chopped (about ½ cup packed)

2 **limes**, cut into small wedges

NOTE: The Red Chile Paste can be made ahead of time. If you're doing everything at once, prepare the paste while the chicken cooks.

RECIPE CONTINUES ➡

SOUPS, SALADS, AND SANDWICHES

3. Add the onions, carrots, and celery to the chicken broth, and cook over medium-low heat until the vegetables are fork-tender, about 15 minutes. Add the chile paste and stir vigorously to incorporate. Add the epazote and season with salt and pepper. Keep warm over very low heat.

4. Pick the meat from the cooled chicken and tear or chop into bite-size pieces. Add it to the pot (reserve the bones for stock, if you like, but discard the skin and cartilage). Increase the heat to medium and simmer for 15 minutes more.

5. To serve, ladle a healthy portion into each large soup bowl. Garnish with a handful of tortilla strips, some avocado, a heavy sprinkling of cilantro, and several lime wedges.

Red Chile Paste

Makes about 1 quart

It may seem like an arduous task to gather all the chiles and spices, but it absolutely makes our tortilla soup. Any leftovers will keep in an airtight container in the fridge for several weeks, or in the freezer almost indefinitely. Use extra paste to flavor your next batch of this soup, to add depth and warming heat to stews, pozole, or a pot of beans, or mix into marinades for meats or vegetables bound for roasting or the grill.

2 **dried guajillo chiles**

2 **dried pasilla chiles**

1 **dried ancho chile**

¼ cup **vegetable oil**

1 small **yellow onion**, chopped

3 **garlic cloves**, chopped

1 teaspoon **ground cumin**

1 teaspoon **ground cinnamon**

1 teaspoon **dried Mexican oregano**

½ teaspoon **ground cloves**

2 tablespoons **tomato paste**

1 **plum tomato**, cored and chopped

1. Place a cast-iron skillet over high heat and toast 2 to 3 chiles at a time, turning once, until they've darkened and blistered all over and puff up; stay close, as this takes less than 1 minute. Transfer to a large bowl and cover with 2 cups of warm water. Place a small plate on top so that the chiles stay submerged. Set aside to rehydrate for 15 minutes.

2. Heat a medium pot over medium-high heat and add the vegetable oil. Toss in the onion and garlic and cook, stirring occasionally, until the onion is soft and translucent, about 3 minutes. Add the cumin, cinnamon, oregano, and cloves, stir to mix, and cook until toasted and fragrant, 2 more minutes. Add the tomato paste and chopped tomato. Cook until the spices are fragrant, an additional 2 minutes.

3. Remove any stems from the rehydrated chiles. Add the chiles and their soaking water to the pot. Bring the liquid to a simmer and let cook, just barely bubbling, to meld the flavors, about 10 minutes.

4. Pour everything into a blender and puree until smooth (Be careful here; if not using a heatproof blender with a very tight-fitting lid, like a Vitamix, allow the chile mixture to cool before blending or work in smaller batches.) Return the puree to the pot and continue to simmer just enough to thicken up a bit, about 10 more minutes.

SPLIT PEA SOUP

Serves 6 to 8

1 pound dried **green split peas**

1 small **onion**, coarsely chopped

1 large **carrot**, coarsely chopped

2 **celery stalks**, coarsely chopped

5 **garlic cloves**

½ cup **olive oil**

½ teaspoon **ground fennel seed**

½ teaspoon **ground coriander**

½ teaspoon **ground cumin**

½ teaspoon **smoked paprika**

3 quarts **vegetable stock** or **water**

Kosher salt and freshly ground **black pepper**

FOR SERVING (OPTIONAL)

Best-quality **olive oil**

Croutons (recipe follows)

NOTE: This recipe calls for the use of a food processor, mostly as a labor saver. If you don't own one, dice the onion, carrot, celery, and garlic as fine as possible.

The term "ugly delicious" gets thrown around in food circles a lot, and for good reason—some of the tastiest things you can eat are true ugly ducklings. Split pea soup is the poster child. With its vaguely army-green color, its thick texture that situates it awkwardly between soup and stew, and its tendency to form a skin on its surface if left alone too long, split pea soup could never win a beauty pageant. But it's only in the looks department that this soup disappoints. Split pea soup is a back-pocket hero—it's stick-to-your-ribs hearty and comes together with ingredients you likely keep in your pantry all the time. Make it before a day on the slopes or a bracing walk in the woods; you'll thank yourself when you get home.

Like most soups, this one benefits from being made in advance, at least a few hours or, better yet, the day before, to let the flavors marry. If, when you go to reheat your soup, you find it has thickened beyond your liking, add warm water or vegetable stock little by little until you achieve the consistency you're looking for.

1. Sort and pick through the peas to remove any stones or debris. Rinse the peas in a colander under cold water. Set aside.

2. In the bowl of a food processor (see Note), combine the onion, carrot, celery, and garlic. Pulse three or four times, a few seconds each time. Scrape down the sides of the bowl with a rubber spatula, then run the processor for 30 additional seconds, until the vegetables are chopped very fine and beginning to stick together (almost like a loose paste).

3. Heat the olive oil in a Dutch oven or large heavy-bottomed saucepan over medium heat. Add the chopped vegetables and sweat them, stirring occasionally, until they turn soft and translucent, 8 to 10 minutes.

4. Increase the heat to high and add the fennel seed, coriander, cumin, and paprika. Toast the spices, stirring constantly to keep them from burning, just until the spices are very fragrant, 2 to 3 minutes.

5. Add the split peas and cover with the vegetable stock. Bring to a boil over high heat. Cook for 5 minutes, then reduce the heat to low and cook, uncovered, stirring occasionally, until the peas are mushy and the soup is thick and creamy, 40 to 50 minutes. Salt while still warm, beginning with a tablespoon and adding more as you like, seasoning with pepper to taste.

6. If you like, serve with a drizzle of good olive oil and a scattering of croutons.

RECIPE CONTINUES ➤➤

Croutons

Makes 2 cups

2 cups day-old **sourdough bread**, cut into small cubes

¼ cup **extra-virgin olive oil**

1 **garlic clove**, finely grated

1 teaspoon **dried thyme**

Kosher salt and freshly ground **black pepper**

1. Preheat the oven to 375°F.

2. Place the bread cubes in a mixing bowl. In a small bowl, whisk together the olive oil, garlic, and thyme. Drizzle the oil mixture over the bread while tossing the cubes to evenly distribute the oil. Season with salt and pepper to taste, toss the bread cubes once more, then spread them evenly on a baking sheet. Bake for 5 minutes. Remove the baking sheet and stir the croutons to ensure they cook evenly. Return the baking sheet to the oven and bake until the croutons are golden brown, an additional 5 to 6 minutes.

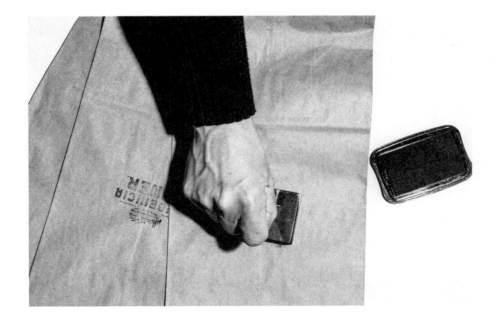

POTATO AND NETTLE SOUP

Serves 8

Kosher salt

2 bunches **stinging nettle tops**, leaves picked (carefully, with gloved hands; see Note, page 109)

½ cup (1 stick, or 4 ounces) **unsalted butter**

1 small **onion**, roughly chopped

2 **celery stalks**, roughly chopped

1 small **leek**, white part only, roughly chopped

3 **Yukon Gold potatoes**, peeled and cut into small chunks

2 **garlic cloves**, roughly chopped

8 cups **vegetable stock**

4 cups **whole milk**

Freshly ground **black pepper**

Best-quality **extra-virgin olive oil**, for serving (optional)

Nettles. Those stinging, burning pains in the neck (or hand, or leg, or whatever body part you happen to brush up against them)! Often found in former barnyards or near abandoned outhouse pits, nettles like to be where humans are (or were). This, Irish food writer Dick Warner put it, "is a one-way attraction."

In the Catskills, nettles are abundant in spring, emerging soon after the thaw. And while they're commonly seen as invasive weeds, they deserve some of our affection in return. As the Irish have long known, nettles are packed with iron, useful as a natural antihistamine, and commonly grow wild (read: free). In Ireland, during the Potato Famine, nettles were gathered as an important nutritional supplement to fend off illness. Earthy and pleasingly bitter, they're a welcome addition to our diets after a winter deprived of fresh greens.

Like most soups, this one is best prepared the day before you plan to serve it. This allows the nettles to mellow and the soup to thicken. Go easy on the salt when preparing the soup—most of the salt you need will come from your vegetable stock—and add more to taste once the flavors have come together.

While late spring, when nettles are still young and tender, is usually cool enough for hot soup, this one takes to chilling quite nicely. Serve as you prefer.

1. Bring a large pot of heavily salted water to a rapid boil over high heat. Make an ice bath by filling a large bowl half full with ice cubes and then adding water just to the level of the ice.

2. Using thick gloves or tongs (to avoid nettle "sting"), drop the nettles into the boiling water and stir to submerge. Maintaining a rapid boil, cook until the nettles are limp and tender and have turned dark green, 5 to 6 minutes. Use a slotted spoon to remove the nettles to the ice bath. Stir the nettles in the ice bath once or twice to stop their cooking. Once the nettles are cool to the touch, remove them from the ice bath and squeeze them thoroughly, using your bare hands or a clean dish towel, to remove excess water. Then roughly chop the nettles—you should have about 1 cup.

RECIPE CONTINUES ➤

3. In a large heavy-bottomed pot, melt the butter over medium heat. Add the onion, celery, leek, potatoes, and garlic. Season with a couple healthy pinches of salt and sweat, stirring occasionally, until the vegetables are tender, 8 to 10 minutes.

4. Add the stock and bring the liquid to a boil. Reduce the heat to medium, then cover the pot. Cook, undisturbed, until the vegetables are meltingly soft, about 20 minutes.

5. Add the milk and chopped nettles to the pot, along with another good pinch of salt and several grinds from the pepper mill. Cook over medium-low heat for another 5 minutes, careful not to raise the soup above a gentle simmer. Turn off the heat and allow the soup to cool for 20 minutes or so. Then, working in batches, puree the soup in a blender until very smooth.

6. Let the soup cool, uncovered, in the fridge, then cover tightly and store in the refrigerator at least 6 hours, and preferably overnight.

7. When you're ready to serve, warm the soup over medium-low heat, adjusting the heat so it doesn't boil. Check for seasoning, adding more salt and fresh pepper to taste. If you like, garnish each serving with a drizzle of good olive oil.

NOTE: The season for harvesting nettles is quite short (once they've developed their tassel-tops and flowers, they become fibrous and gritty), but like many greens, they freeze well. To have access to their unique flavor and nutrient density all year long, simply follow the steps for blanching, draining, and wringing out the nettles, then freeze in plastic freezer bags.

CORN CHOWDER

Serves 8

FOR THE BASE

½ cup (1 stick)
unsalted butter

1 large **onion**, roughly
chopped

2 **celery stalks**,
roughly chopped

2 cups **corn kernels**,
fresh or frozen

2 large **Yukon Gold
potatoes**, peeled and
roughly chopped

2 **garlic cloves**,
minced

Kosher salt

8 cups **vegetable
stock**

1 sprig of **fresh thyme**

1 dried **bay leaf**

4 cups **whole milk**

Freshly ground
black pepper

TO FINISH

1 large **onion**, cut into
small cubes

2 **celery stalks**,
thinly sliced

2 medium **carrots**,
cut into small cubes

2 cups **corn kernels**,
fresh or frozen

2 large **Yukon Gold
potatoes**, peeled and
cut into small cubes

2 tablespoons
chopped **fresh chives**

Corn chowder is one of those teases of a dish: a sunny reminder of high summer that's mostly eaten as farm produce dwindles for the season. But if you find yourself with a cool day during corn season, do yourself a favor and make a batch of this soup. Fresh corn and newly dug potatoes are inimitable pleasures of high harvest season.

Unlike some chowders—which make use of heavy cream for richness—this one uses only whole milk. Rather than having tons of fat, this recipe relies heavily on pureed vegetables for its silkiness and body, making for a lighter soup.

The sugars in corn kernels begin turning to starch the moment an ear of corn is picked from the stalk, so if you can't find *very* fresh corn on the cob, frozen kernels are a better bet. If you're buying corn at a farmers market or farmstand, ask for the most recently picked ears—ideally no earlier than the morning they're being sold. You may feel like a picky snob, but you'll be richly rewarded with superior flavor.

1. **Make the base:** Melt the butter in a large heavy-bottomed pot over medium heat. Add the onion, celery, corn, potatoes, and garlic. Season lightly with salt, and sweat until the vegetables are tender, 8 to 10 minutes.

2. Add the stock, thyme, and bay leaf and bring to a boil over high heat. Reduce the heat to medium and cover the pot. Cook until the vegetables are meltingly soft, about 20 minutes.

3. Remove the bay leaf and thyme, then add the milk. In a blender, working in batches if needed, carefully puree the liquid and vegetables until smooth. Return the soup base to the pot and season with salt and pepper.

4. **To finish:** Add the onion, celery, carrots, corn, and potatoes to the soup base. Simmer, uncovered, until the vegetables are tender, 12 to 15 minutes. Season again with salt and pepper. Garnish with the chives and serve.

Esopus
Oliverea
BM
1428
C A T S K I L L P A R K
(STATE FOREST PRESERVE)
Hollow
River
Spring
460 000 FEET
27'30"
FROST VALLEY 3 MI.
(PEEKAMOOSE MOUNTAIN)
6167 IV NW
548
25'
549
SCALE 1:24 000
1 MILE
1000 0 1000 2000 3000 4000 5000 6000 7000 FEET
1 KILOMETER
CONTOUR INTERVAL 20 FEET
DATUM IS MEAN SEA LEVEL
MN
GN
12°
213 MILS
0°23'
7 MILS
my Map Service
ned by the Geological Survey
d USC&GS
ial photographs by photogrammetric
otographs taken 1943. Field check 1945
e Geological Survey 1960
1927 North American datum
NEW YORK

KALE AND WHITE BEAN SOUP

Serves 6 to 8

This soup is a cinch to pull together but hearty enough to stave off the cold and winds that blow through the Catskills all winter long. Like many soups, this one benefits from sitting for a few hours—better yet, overnight—before serving. What's more, allowing the soup to cool and then reheating it will encourage the beans to begin to break down a bit, adding body and thickness to the soup.

1. Sort and pick through the beans to remove any rocks, mud, or other debris. Rinse the beans in a colander under cold water.

2. Place the beans in a large bowl and cover with water at least three times the volume of the beans. Stir the beans a few times and remove any stray bits that rise to the top of the water. Cover the bowl with a lid or plate and set on the counter to soak overnight.

3. The next day, heat the olive oil in a large pot over medium-high heat. Add the onion, carrot, celery, and garlic. Cook, stirring occasionally, until the vegetables are soft, 8 to 10 minutes.

4. Drain the beans and add them to the pot along with the stock, rosemary, thyme, and bay leaves. Bring the liquid to a boil and cook uncovered for 5 minutes. Reduce the heat to medium-low and cook, uncovered, until the beans are soft, 25 to 30 minutes.

5. Add the kale, salt, and pepper. Cover the pot and cook until the kale is tender, 8 to 10 minutes. Serve the soup sprinkled with the parmesan cheese and, if you like, with slices of warm crusty bread.

1 pound small dried **white beans**, such as navy, cannellini, or great northern

¼ cup **olive oil**

1 large **onion**, diced

2 medium **carrots**, diced

3 **celery stalks**, diced

6 **garlic cloves**, minced

12 cups **vegetable stock**

1 sprig of **fresh rosemary**, leaves picked and finely chopped

1 sprig of **fresh thyme**, leaves picked and finely chopped

2 dried **bay leaves**

1 bunch **lacinato (Tuscan or dinosaur) kale**, stemmed and roughly chopped

2 tablespoons **kosher salt**

2 teaspoons freshly ground **black pepper**

2 cups grated **parmesan cheese**

Crusty bread, warmed, for serving (optional)

BRUNSWICK STEW

Serves 6 to 8

When it comes to Brunswick stew's origin story, the jury's still out: the stew was either born on an 1828 hunting expedition in Brunswick County, Virginia, or in 1898 on St. Simon's Island near Brunswick, Georgia. Today, historical quibbles aside, Brunswick stew is as prevalent and varied in the American South as barbecue. Across the region, you're bound to find variations on a basic theme: small mammals (traditionally wild game), corn, and beans thickened with tomatoes and cooked down, as it's been said, until the paddle can stand up in the middle.

Though virtually unknown in these parts, Brunswick stew is as suited to the Catskills as it is to the rural South, with our shared cultures of hunting and farming. Chef Chris makes his Brunswick stew the North Carolina way, with a mix of chicken and pork.

1. In a Dutch oven or other large heavy-bottomed pot with a lid, heat ¼ cup of the olive oil over high heat until it just begins to smoke. Add the pork and cook, stirring occasionally, until well browned, about 10 minutes. Transfer the pork to a plate and set aside. Add the remaining ¼ cup olive oil to the pot and brown the chicken, stirring occasionally, about 8 minutes.

2. Add the pork back to the pot and reduce the heat to medium. Add the onions and garlic, season lightly with salt and pepper, and stir. Continue to cook, stirring occasionally, until the onions and garlic are translucent, about 5 minutes.

3. Add the tomato paste and thyme and stir for just long enough to cook out the raw taste of the tomato paste, 20 to 30 seconds. Pour in the diced tomatoes (including the juices), vinegar, barbecue sauce, and chicken broth, and give a quick stir. Turn the heat up to high and bring just to a boil, then reduce the heat to medium-low and cover. Cook, stirring occasionally, until the stew has thickened and the meat flakes apart with a fork, about 2½ hours.

4. Add the lima beans, corn, and Tabasco sauce, and season again with salt and pepper. Cook until the vegetables are fork-tender, another 10 minutes. Serve hot.

½ cup **olive oil**

1 pound **boneless pork stew meat** (shoulder or butt), cut into 1-inch cubes

1 pound **boneless, skinless chicken thighs**, cut into 1-inch cubes

2 large **onions**, roughly chopped (about 4 cups)

7 **garlic cloves**, roughly chopped

Kosher salt and freshly ground **black pepper**

1 tablespoon **tomato paste**

1 teaspoon chopped **fresh thyme leaves**

1 (14-ounce) can **diced tomatoes**

1 tablespoon **apple cider vinegar**

1 cup **barbecue sauce** (best quality you can find)

2 cups **low-sodium chicken broth**

2 cups **lima beans**, fresh or frozen

2 cups **corn kernels**, fresh or frozen

2 teaspoons **Tabasco sauce**

The Grand Resorts and Bungalows of the Catskills

The wreckage hides in plain sight. Empty swimming pools tattooed with graffiti and tangled with vines, old lawn chairs splintered and moss covered, and vast empty buildings that once promised escape, respite, and in some cases, extreme luxury. These are the remains of the Catskills' heyday as a prominent tourist destination. They dot Ulster and Greene Counties and create a veritable web across Sullivan County, the mid-century heart of the region's tourism, reminding us of what was.

From its grand resorts to modest bungalow colonies, the Catskills region has long been a destination. If you've ever seen *Dirty Dancing*, you can conjure a pretty good image in your mind's eye. It's all lakes and woods, dappled light and lazy afternoons, dances and à la carte dining.

What happened?

Back up. The Catskills' first economic boom came in the early 1800s, largely from lumber and tanning industries. As forests were cut down (lumbering required, of course, the felling of trees, and tanning hides depended upon the bark of the regionally abundant hemlock tree), those industries crashed. Many families left, leaving both the land and the towns largely empty. Vacant spaces made way for dairy and poultry farming

in the 1880s, which capitalized on the newly cleared pasture and meadowland. Seasonal farm laborers and traders moved through the region, often renting rooms in farmhouses for their stays. Some industrious farmers saw the opportunity to supplement their income, expanding to bungalow colonies and even small hotels. Such was the seed for the area's travel industry.

As roads and railroads improved the region's links to increasingly industrial New York City, advertising helped lure outdoor enthusiasts, artists, and tuberculosis patients (the area had a wealth of sanitoriums) north to take advantage of the Catskills' fresh air and rolling landscape. But by the dawn of the First World War in the early twentieth century, overspeculation led to another crash.

By the 1920s, the number of Jewish immigrants from Eastern Europe and Russia had increased dramatically in New York City, as had anti-Semitism. Jewish entrepreneurs— most famously Asher Selig Grossinger—saw an opportunity to provide places for Jews to gather together safely to practice their cultural traditions and foster social ties. It also provided a space for Jews to assimilate by practicing a particularly American pastime: vacationing.

The "Borscht Belt," also known as the "Jewish Alps," saw its tourist heyday in the economically prosperous but socially tenuous decades of the 1950s and '60s. At its height, Ulster and Sullivan Counties boasted more than 50,000 bungalows and 538 hotels. In the wake of World War II, Jews had flocked to the southern edge of the Catskills seeking community, hoping to reassert the social and cultural bonds that were so deeply threatened by the war's horrific unfolding. The Borscht Belt hoteliers invited levity via entertainment, courting entertainers like Lenny Bruce, Jerry Lewis, Joan Rivers, and Woody Allen. For a time, the Borscht Belt held its own against major cities like New York, Los Angeles, and Chicago as a hub not only of Jewish culture but also a forecaster of American culture more broadly. The most deluxe resorts offered the latest in leisure: In 1958, Grossinger's unveiled a massive indoor pool flanked by ultra-luxurious amenities. In the following seasons, neighboring resorts stretched way beyond their financial means to keep up. No expense was spared to draw first-time visitors and to retain guests season after season. But the one-upmanship wouldn't last.

The 1960s brought change to the Catskills, as they did everywhere else in American life. The spending power of the postwar era waned, railroad service to the Catskills dropped off, and airfares became more affordable; Europe and the Caribbean beckoned. Air-conditioning made the prospect of summers in the city less daunting. And, as the fresh wounds of the war and the witch hunts of the McCarthy era scabbed over, a younger generation of American Jews entered the mainstream.

Other groups, too, were feeling the changes. While most famously the Catskills resorts catered to New York Jews, bungalow colonies and inns throughout the region were ethnically themed, drawing enclaves of Irish, Italian, and Polish Americans, among others. Although far from integrated, the region's tourism industry was remarkably diverse.

As the peaceful postwar years settled in, and a national movement toward racial and ethnic desegregation began, the fashion of culturally specific vacations began to fade. Resorts, hotels, and bungalow colonies folded like dominoes in the 1970s and '80s, and the Catskills region as a whole faltered. Today, some of the resorts have been repurposed as retreat centers or even private estates, but many languish, neglected if not forgotten.

Recently, though, innovation in tourism has returned to the region. Entrepreneurs are breathing new life into what were once considered tear-down properties and repurposing industrial and agricultural spaces to accommodate the growing number of visitors who are, once again, flocking to the region. From upscale tenting to luxurious resorts like the Emerson Resort and Spa, rustic-chic private homes to charmingly kitschy roadside motels like the nearby Graham & Co. and Spruceton Inn, the winding roads of the Catskills once again lead to myriad escapes from the hustle of workaday lives. Sullivan County has even seen the arrival of a major casino development, aptly named the Resorts World Catskills.

While times and demographics have shifted, nostalgia has a leading role in what has emerged in the Catskills of late. As Marisa Scheinfeld wrote in her 2016 book, *The Borscht Belt,* looking back at the Golden Era of the region isn't merely "an archival adventure into the past"; it's also a "journey into an unruly present and future."

SMOKED SALMON SALAD
WITH ASPARAGUS, CUCUMBER, AND DILL-CAPER VINAIGRETTE

Serves 6 to 8

FOR THE DILL-CAPER VINAIGRETTE

⅓ cup **fresh lemon juice** (from about 2 lemons)

2 tablespoons **white wine vinegar**

2 tablespoons **Dijon mustard**

1 cup **extra-virgin olive oil**

¼ cup **capers**, drained and roughly chopped

¼ cup finely chopped **fresh dill**

1 teaspoon **kosher salt**

½ teaspoon freshly ground **black pepper**

FOR THE SALAD

1 bunch fresh **asparagus**, trimmed

1 tablespoon **extra-virgin olive oil**

Kosher salt and freshly ground **black pepper**

1 pound **baby spinach**

1 cup diced **seedless cucumber**

3 **French breakfast radishes**, thinly shaved

1 pound **hot smoked salmon**

Spring comes late in these parts. Here, mud season sticks around a long time, often bringing with it late snows and dashed hopes for warmer weather. When spring finally comes to the Catskills, though, we do everything we can to herald the arrival of green things. Among the first treats of the season are tender young spinach; small, spicy radishes; and, perhaps most exciting of all, pencil-thin asparagus. Here, they're showcased together with some classic New York City flavors like briny capers, smoked salmon, and dill. Everything is given an extra dose of brightness with a lemony vinaigrette. It's like a fully loaded bagel on a diet or the feeling of freedom you get when you finally put away your winter coat for good.

1. **Make the vinaigrette:** Place the lemon juice, vinegar, and mustard in a mixing bowl and whisk to combine. Slowly drizzle in the olive oil while whisking to emulsify the vinaigrette. It should look creamy and smooth, with some droplets of oil still floating on the surface. Add the capers, dill, salt, and pepper and whisk again to mix everything well. Place the vinaigrette in the fridge to keep cool while assembling the other ingredients. (It will keep refrigerated in a sealed container for up to 1 week.)

2. Preheat the oven to 450°F.

3. **Make the salad:** Place the asparagus on a roasting or baking sheet and drizzle with the olive oil. Season the asparagus lightly with salt and pepper. Roast until lightly browned and tender but still firm, about 7 minutes. Remove the pan from the oven and set aside to cool. Once the asparagus has cooled to room temperature, cut the spears into 1-inch pieces.

4. Assemble the salad by placing the asparagus, baby spinach, cucumber, and radishes in a large bowl. Pour the dressing over the salad, season with salt and pepper, and toss to mix. Break the salmon into bite-size pieces over the top of the salad and toss again to distribute the salmon evenly. Serve immediately.

WATERMELON AND FETA SALAD
WITH BASIL-BALSAMIC VINAIGRETTE
Serves 6

Many people envision watermelon salad as big hunks of watermelon and just a sprinkling of crumbled cheese and maybe some herbs for garnish. This isn't that. Rather, this is a chopped salad, refreshing and high on crunch—the sort you don't see much anymore in this age of ubiquitous leafy-green worship.

Truth is, in high summer, when temperatures in the Northeast rise and we can go weeks on end without rain, farmers can't grow lettuces—they burn and wilt in the heat or bolt immediately and become utterly unpalatable. Only a few salad greens with a little backbone, like the arugula we use here, can stand the heat, *if* they're grown fast and picked while still young.

· ·

1. Make the vinaigrette: Place the basil, olive oil, and garlic in a blender and pulse on high speed until the basil is finely chopped and the mixture forms a smooth paste. Add the vinegar and ¼ cup water and blend again until the vinaigrette is emulsified, about 10 seconds. Season lightly with salt and pepper and stir (be judicious with the salt, as the feta adds much of the saltiness this salad needs).

2. Make the salad: Place the watermelon, feta, cucumber, tomatoes, and red onion in a large bowl and dress with the vinaigrette. Toss everything to evenly coat and allow to marinate for at least 5 minutes, but no longer than 30 minutes. Add the arugula to the bowl, check the seasoning, adding salt and pepper to your taste, and toss again. Serve immediately.

FOR THE BASIL-BALSAMIC VINAIGRETTE

1 bunch **fresh basil**, leaves picked and rough chopped

1 cup **extra-virgin olive oil**

1 **garlic clove**, minced

½ cup **balsamic vinegar**

Kosher salt and freshly ground **black pepper**

FOR THE SALAD

4 cups diced **seedless watermelon** (½- to ¾-inch cubes)

2 cups diced **feta cheese** (½- to ¾-inch cubes)

1 cup **seedless (English hothouse) cucumber**, sliced down the middle, then each half halved again, and cut into small pieces (see Note)

1 pint **cherry tomatoes**, halved

1 small **red onion**, halved and thinly sliced

½ pound **baby arugula**

Kosher salt and freshly ground **black pepper**

NOTE: The goal with the chopped elements here is to keep them as uniform in size as possible. We recommend a ½-inch or ¾-inch dice, but you don't need to be too fussy about it. Just try to keep the feta, cuke, and watermelon roughly the same size; a halved cherry tomato makes for a nice gauge.

FOR THE BEETS

2 pounds large **red beets**, washed, tops and bottoms trimmed

2 sprigs of **fresh thyme**

Kosher salt

3 tablespoons **sherry vinegar**

2 tablespoons **extra-virgin olive oil**

1 tablespoon **granulated sugar**

Freshly ground **black pepper**

FOR THE SALAD

10 ounces **baby kale**

1 seedless **(English hothouse) cucumber**, diced

3 **French breakfast radishes**, shaved very thin (a mandoline is helpful here)

Yogurt Dressing (recipe follows)

Kosher salt and freshly ground **black pepper**

1 cup **whole almonds**, toasted and roughly chopped

½ cup thinly sliced **scallions**, green and white parts

4 **hard-boiled eggs** (see page 29), cubed or sliced

ROASTED BEET AND KALE SALAD
WITH YOGURT DRESSING
Serves 6 to 8

While kale is commonly thought of as virtuous, this salad—inspired by chilled borscht—is playful. Big on color and flavor, made hearty by the greens, marinated beets, and a creamy yogurt dressing, it's a meal unto itself.

This salad makes for a terrific weeknight dinner or take-to-work salad, as the beets and dressing can be made ahead of time and kept in the fridge for up to a week. The same goes for the hard-boiled eggs. When you're ready to eat, all you need to do is chop up the few remaining vegetables and a handful of nuts, and you're good to go.

1. Preheat the oven to 375°F.

2. Place the beets in a Dutch oven along with the thyme sprigs. Season the beets with 2 tablespoons salt and add water to a depth of 2 inches. Cover the pot tightly with aluminum foil and then cover with the lid.

3. Roast the beets until a knife inserted into the center meets little to no resistance, 1 to 1½ hours, depending upon the size of your beets. (Use caution when removing the lid and foil to test the beets, as a blast of steam will rapidly escape from the pot.) When the beets are fully cooked, let cool, uncovered, until they are still warm, but cool enough to handle.

4. Gently rub the skins off the beets using a paper towel. Cut the peeled beets into small cubes and place in a bowl. Add the sherry vinegar, olive oil, and sugar, and toss to marinate the beets. Season the beets with salt and pepper and place, covered, in the refrigerator to chill for a minimum of an hour or up to a week.

5. When you're ready to eat, assemble the salad. Place the kale, beets, cucumbers, and radishes in a large salad bowl. Pour a generous amount of the yogurt dressing over the top and season with salt and pepper to taste. Toss to coat everything with the dressing, adding more if you like, then top with the almonds, scallions, and chopped egg. Serve immediately.

RECIPE CONTINUES ➤

Yogurt Dressing

Makes about 1½ cups

1 cup plain **whole-milk Greek yogurt**

½ cup **extra-virgin olive oil**

1 small **garlic clove**, minced

2 tablespoons **fresh lemon juice**

1 tablespoon **apple cider vinegar**

½ teaspoon **kosher salt**, plus more
    to taste

1. Place the yogurt, olive oil, garlic, lemon juice, vinegar, salt, and ½ cup water in a bowl and whisk vigorously until the olive oil is fully incorporated and the dressing has the consistency of slightly thickened cream. Adjust the consistency of the dressing to your liking with more water, adding just a few drops at a time.

2. Season with salt to taste, and set aside or store in the fridge. (The dressing will keep, covered and refrigerated, for up to 1 week.)

BLACK-EYED PEA AND THREE-PEPPER SALAD

Serves 6 to 8 as a side

Bean salads can feel boring, like the worst kind of from-a-can "cooking." Who hasn't had an utterly unpalatable three-bean salad from a salad bar? We're here to undo the negative association. Salads based on beans—or "peas," as Southerners are prone to calling them—are filling, satisfying, and incredibly versatile. This salad is a (vegan) favorite that plays nicely alongside grilled meat, poultry, and fish, or makes a great lunch all on its own. Unlike a lot of salads, this one can hold at room temp just fine for a while. It may quickly become your go-to for potlucks, picnics, or the base for a satisfying make-ahead lunch.

1. Sort and pick through the peas to remove any rocks, mud, or other debris. Rinse the peas in a colander under cold water.

2. Place the peas in large bowl and cover with cool water at least three times the volume of the peas. Stir the peas a few times and remove any stray bits that rise to the top of the water. Cover the bowl with a lid or plate and set on the counter overnight.

3. The next day, drain the peas and place in a large pot. Add enough fresh water to cover the top of the peas by 3 inches, about 3 quarts. Bring to a rapid boil over high heat (the water will be bubbling vigorously and the peas, swirling in the pot). Boil for 5 minutes, then reduce the heat to medium-low and cook until the peas are tender, 25 to 30 minutes (the time will vary depending on how old your peas are; fresher dried beans, lentils,

or peas of any kind contain more moisture). Remove the peas from the heat, season with salt (start with about 1 tablespoon, as you can add more later), and let stand, uncovered, for 30 minutes.

4. Drain the peas in a colander and shake as much of the water out as possible. Place them in a medium bowl and add the lemon juice and olive oil. Stir everything to combine. Check for salt, adding more to your liking. Set aside to cool to room temperature. (Stop here if you're making these peas ahead of time; refrigerate the peas until you're ready to finish the salad.)

5. Once the peas are cool (or, if you've prepared them beforehand, you're ready to eat), stir in the red onion, bell peppers, jalapeño, scallions, and cilantro (if using). Season with salt and pepper and serve.

---

1 pound dried **black-eyed peas** (see Note)

Kosher salt

½ cup **fresh lemon juice** (from 3 to 4 lemons)

½ cup **extra-virgin olive oil**

1 small **red onion**, cut into small dice

1 **green bell pepper**, seeded, cored, and cut into small dice

1 **red bell pepper**, seeded, cored, and cut into small dice

1 **jalapeño pepper**, seeded and finely chopped

¼ cup chopped **scallions**, green and white parts

⅓ cup chopped **fresh cilantro** (optional)

Freshly ground **black pepper**

NOTE: The beans can be prepared a day or two ahead of time, but don't wait to dress them with the lemon juice and olive oil—always dress bean and grain salads warm, as flavors and fats will be absorbed more fully, so your salad will taste more consistent throughout. But wait to add the vegetables, onion, and cilantro until ready to serve, so they retain their crunch and vibrant color.

1 cup **whole-milk ricotta**

¼ cup grated **parmesan cheese**

1 teaspoon grated **lemon zest**

½ tablespoon chopped **fresh chives**

2½ tablespoons chopped **fresh parsley**

Kosher salt and freshly ground **black pepper**

4 thick slices **rustic sourdough bread**, such as pain de campagne, levain, or miche, toasted

1 tablespoon **unsalted butter**

4 large **eggs**

Mushroom Gravy (recipe follows), warmed

'SHROOMS ON A SHINGLE
(A.K.A. MUSHROOM-SMOTHERED TOAST WITH HERBED RICOTTA)

Serves 4

Like its namesake, the military mainstay "shit on a shingle," our 'shrooms on a shingle is homely in appearance. But unlike its dispiriting relative, this open-faced sandwich is a joy to eat: basic ingredients layered atop one another for outsize flavor. This deceptively hearty dish—a ricotta-topped toast that's smothered in fresh mushroom gravy and finished off with a fried egg—is a complete meal in itself, though a crunchy salad served alongside would add welcome brightness and fend off any giggle-inducing comparisons.

1. Place the ricotta, parmesan, lemon zest, chives, and ½ tablespoon parsley in a medium bowl. Season with salt and pepper and whisk until smooth. Spread the toast generously with the herbed ricotta.

2. In a large nonstick pan, heat the butter over medium-high heat and cook your eggs sunny-side up (see page 29).

3. Smother each toast slice with a cup of warm mushroom gravy and top with an egg. Finish with salt, pepper, and remaining 2 tablespoons parsley, and serve.

RECIPE CONTINUES ➤

Mushroom Gravy

Makes 4 cups

Here in the Catskills, we're right in the thick of wild mushroom territory. Generous friends have brought in crates full of foraged mushrooms— king oysters, morels, and hen of the woods. We're lucky that way. With mushrooms this fresh, a chef's only job is to shine the spotlight on their inherent earthy goodness. As our culture and customers grow more and more health-conscious, mushrooms offer hearty satisfaction without meat.

This recipe, which results in a thick, coating gravy, is almost vegan and could be adapted as such by substituting olive oil for the butter in the final sautéing step.

½ ounce **dried shiitakes**

¼ cup plus 2 tablespoons **olive oil**

½ pound **fresh button mushrooms**, rinsed and sliced

½ pound **fresh shiitake mushrooms**, stemmed and sliced

1 small **onion**, thinly sliced

2 **garlic cloves**, minced

2 ounces **sweet vermouth**, **Madeira**, or other nutty fortified wine

Kosher salt and freshly ground **black pepper**

1½ teaspoons **unsalted butter**

1 sprig of **fresh thyme**, leaves picked

1. Place the dried shiitakes in a large pot and add 3 cups water. Bring to a boil over high heat, then reduce to medium-low and simmer for 15 minutes. Remove from the heat and let steep for 30 minutes.

2. Meanwhile, in a large heavy-bottomed stockpot or Dutch oven, heat ¼ cup of the olive oil over high heat. Add half the button and fresh shiitake mushrooms, half the sliced onion, and the minced garlic, and cook, stirring frequently, until well browned, being careful not to singe the garlic, 7 to 10 minutes. Add the vermouth and scrape up any caramelized bits from the pan with a wooden spoon. Season with salt and pepper and cook until the liquid has completely evaporated.

3. Strain the dried shiitake broth, reserving the rehydrated shiitakes for another use. (Avoid the temptation to incorporate them into the gravy, as they add an unwanted bitterness. Instead, save them to toss into salads or a stir-fry.) Add all the mushroom broth to the sautéed mushrooms. Bring to a boil over high heat, then reduce the heat to medium-low and allow to cook, uncovered, until the liquid has reduced by about one-fourth, about 30 minutes. Remove from the heat and allow to cool slightly. Pour the gravy into a blender and process until smooth; the texture will be gloopy at this point, similar to a canned mushroom soup concentrate. Season again with salt and black pepper, transfer back to the pot, and keep warm over low heat.

4. In a sauté pan, heat the remaining 2 tablespoons of olive oil over high heat. Add the remaining button and shiitake mushrooms and the remaining onion. Cook over high heat for 5 minutes, stirring occasionally, until the onion is dark brown, has caramelized slightly, and gives off a deep earthy fragrance. Add the butter and thyme, and cook until the mushrooms and onion are deeply browned and caramelized, about 5 minutes more. Season with salt and pepper. Add the caramelized mushrooms and onion to the warm mushroom puree. Use immediately or allow to cool completely and keep, in an airtight container, for up to 1 week (to reheat, warm over low heat and stir occasionally).

3 (5-ounce) cans **albacore tuna** packed in water (we use Wild Planet)

½ small **red onion**, finely chopped (about ¼ cup)

2 **celery stalks**, finely chopped (about ½ cup)

1 ripe **avocado**

½ cup **mayonnaise**

1 tablespoon **Dijon mustard**

1 tablespoon **fresh lemon juice**, plus more to taste

Kosher salt and freshly ground **black pepper**

8 slices of **bread** (preferably rye or whole wheat), toasted

4 crisp **lettuce leaves** (such as green or red leaf, romaine, or Boston)

1 large (beefsteak) ripe **tomato**, cored and sliced

MITCHELL'S TUNA AND AVOCADO SALAD SANDWICHES

Serves 4

Every diner needs a tuna salad sandwich. It's comforting, unfussy, and all-American. Ours is enriched with avocado for extra creaminess, cut through with bits of celery, red onion, a little mustard, and some lemon juice. The sandwich is named in honor of Mike's late father-in-law, Mitchell, whose standing order at his local New York City diner was a tuna salad sandwich and a Coke.

1. Drain the tuna in a colander and gently break up to remove any excess water. Place in a medium bowl and add the red onion and celery.

2. In another medium bowl, combine the avocado, mayonnaise, mustard, and lemon juice. Use a potato masher or metal whisk to mix the ingredients until the avocado breaks down into a smooth, creamy paste.

3. Add the avocado mayonnaise to the tuna and gently stir to combine without turning the tuna into mush. Season with salt and pepper.

4. Divide the tuna salad among 4 of the bread slices, and top with a lettuce leaf, several tomato slices, and the second slice of toast. Serve immediately. (This is best eaten the same day you prepare it, as the avocado oxidizes a bit.)

PIMENTO CHEESE PATTY MELTS

Serves 4

The patty melt, which is said to have originated in William "Tiny" Naylor's restaurants in Southern California, is pure Americana. With the heft and satisfaction of a cheeseburger, browned onions for sweetness, and the crunch of grilled cheese, they tick every pleasure box.

When Chef Chris put this on the menu, he substituted pimento cheese for the traditional Swiss or cheddar. Pimento cheese is a sandwich and hors d'oeuvre staple throughout the American South that is tragically underappreciated in these northern parts. Here, the tangy pimientos and warming spices cut through the rich fat of the sandwich. The cheddar cheese gets perfectly melty and binds to the onions, and the mayo and cream cheese keep things extra luscious. While you could certainly tack on condiments here if you wanted, there's no need—this is a fully loaded sandwich all on its own.

3 tablespoons **vegetable oil**

1 large **onion**, halved and thinly sliced

Kosher salt and freshly ground **black pepper**

1½ pounds **ground beef** (80 or 90% lean), divided into 4 (6-ounce) patties, each ½ to ¾ inch thick

½ cup (1 stick) **unsalted butter**, softened

8 slices **rye bread**

Pimento Cheese (recipe follows)

1. In a large heavy skillet, heat 2 tablespoons of the oil over high heat. Add the sliced onion and cook, stirring frequently, until the onion begins to brown, about 5 minutes. Season lightly with salt and a sprinkle of fresh pepper. Reduce the heat to low and cook until the onion is a deep caramel brown, another 10 minutes. Transfer the onion to a bowl or plate and set aside. Wipe the skillet clean with a paper towel and return to the stove.

2. Season the hamburger patties liberally with salt and pepper. In the skillet, heat the remaining 1 tablespoon oil over high heat, just until it begins to smoke. Gently lay the patties in the skillet and press down with a spatula until the patties are about ¼ inch thick and roughly the same size as your pieces of bread. Cook undisturbed until the patties are well browned and begin to char and crisp, about 2 minutes. Flip the burgers with a spatula and cook until browned on the other side, about another 2 minutes. Remove the patties to a plate.

RECIPE CONTINUES ➥

3. Carefully wipe out the skillet and return to the stove over medium-high heat. Spread 1 tablespoon butter on each slice of rye bread, making sure to spread it completely over the slice. Place 4 slices, buttered side down, into the skillet and top each with about ¼ cup of pimento cheese. Top each with a burger and divide the caramelized onion among the 4 patties. Spread another healthy spoonful of pimento cheese on the remaining slices of rye (opposite side from the butter) and place on top of the burgers, pressing down to seal. Cook until the bottom slice is golden brown, 1 to 2 minutes. Flip the sandwiches and cook until the other side is golden brown, about 2 minutes more. Serve immediately.

Pimento Cheese

Makes 2 cups

8 ounces **sharp cheddar cheese**, grated (about 2 cups)

½ cup (4 ounces, or ½ a standard brick) **cream cheese**, softened

¼ cup **mayonnaise**

1 cup **pimientos**, thoroughly drained and finely chopped

½ teaspoon **sweet Spanish paprika**

½ teaspoon **garlic powder**

½ teaspoon **white pepper**

½ teaspoon **kosher salt**

Pinch of **cayenne**

Place the cheddar, cream cheese, mayonnaise, pimientos, paprika, garlic powder, white pepper, salt, and cayenne in a large bowl and, using a wooden spoon, mix thoroughly until all the ingredients are well combined. Use immediately (or cover and keep in the fridge for up to a week; see Note).

NOTE: Pimento cheese is the standout ingredient for this sandwich, but don't relegate your consumption of it to this dish. Spread the leftovers from this recipe on crackers or use in lieu of peanut butter with celery. It's a terrifically addictive snack. It keeps for up to a week, covered, in the fridge. Just pull it out half an hour before using so the spread can soften up a bit.

THE PHOENICIA DINER GUIDE TO STACKING THE PERFECT TURKEY CLUB

We hear a lot about this sandwich, about how impossibly large it is, and questions about how could you possibly open your mouth wide enough to take a real bite. While we won't tell you how to eat it (watching people come up with their own style of tackling a turkey club is good fun), we will tell you how to make it:

Lay out 3 slices of well-toasted bread. Give each slice a generous slick of mayo. On 2 of the slices, you're going to make stacks: first, 4 or 5 thin slices of roast turkey breast on each stack, then 2 slices of bacon, 1 nice thick slice of tomato, and a layer of crunchy lettuce (we like romaine). Now you have 2 simple stacks and 1 mayo-slathered piece of toast.

Take the single slice of toast and flip it over, mayo side down, on top of one of the stacks. Now you've got a "single-decker" sandwich, and a topless stack. To make it a club, use two hands to pick up the single-decker sandwich you just made, and lay it carefully on top of the other stack.

Now you've got to hold it all together. Insert 4 (6-inch) sandwich toothpicks (these come in frilled and paddle varieties; take your pick), making a cross or plus sign (think the four points of the compass)—one on each side of the sandwich, about ¼ inch in from the crust, pressing down with one hand while pushing the toothpick all the way through with the other. Then, using a sharp, non-serrated knife, slice from corner to corner, making 4 triangles with a toothpick in the center of each.

Using one hand to hold the tip of the toothpick and the other to support the base piece of bread, use the toothpick to tilt each quarter backward, laying it on its uncut side. Press the tip of the toothpick the rest of the way through, so it pokes out of the bottom piece of toast. Repeat with the other three quarters, and serve.

GRILLED LAMB PITAS
WITH CARROT-MINT SLAW AND CUCUMBER YOGURT

Serves 4

FOR THE LAMB

1 pound **boneless leg of lamb**

Kosher salt and freshly ground **black pepper**

¼ cup **olive oil**

2 **garlic cloves**, minced

2 teaspoons chopped **fresh rosemary**

1 teaspoon **fresh thyme leaves**

1 teaspoon chopped **fresh oregano**

½ teaspoon grated **lemon zest**

FOR THE CARROT-MINT SLAW

1 or 2 medium **carrots**, coarsely grated (about 1 cup)

2 tablespoons chopped **fresh mint**

1 tablespoon **olive oil**

2 teaspoons **fresh lemon juice**

1 teaspoon **honey**

Kosher salt and freshly ground **black pepper**

This dish is a nod to Greek diners everywhere, where you often find Mediterranean specialties scattered throughout an otherwise all-American menu. Gyro is one of our favorites: a thick, fluffy pita wrapped around grilled meat and dressed with tzatziki and chopped fresh vegetables. It's an incredibly satisfying sandwich, one that's become harder and harder to find in these parts.

Here, we stay quite true to the classic, piling pita with grilled lamb and topping it with cool yogurt dressing, chopped tomatoes, and romaine—and a little extra crunch from a minted carrot slaw.

1. **Marinate the lamb:** Place the lamb in a large baking dish, and season all sides with salt and pepper. In a small bowl, mix the olive oil, garlic, rosemary, thyme, oregano, and lemon zest. Stir to combine, then pour over the lamb. Place in the fridge to marinate for at least 1 hour, or up to overnight (if marinating the lamb for more than 2 hours, cover loosely with plastic wrap).

2. **Make the slaw:** While your lamb is marinating (or the next day, if you're marinating overnight), place the grated carrot in a medium bowl and add the mint, olive oil, lemon juice, and honey. Season with salt and pepper and stir again. Place in the fridge to keep cool until the lamb is ready. (Slaw will keep for 3 days refrigerated.)

3. **Make the yogurt:** In another medium bowl, stir together the yogurt, cucumber, dill, and lemon juice, then season with salt and pepper. Refrigerate while you cook the lamb.

4. Heat your grill to medium-high heat. Remove the lamb from the fridge. Using one hand, remove the meat from the marinade and use your other hand to gently rub off excess olive oil. Place the lamb on the grill. Cook on one side, making sure to avoid burning the meat by moving it to cooler spots if there are flare-ups from dripping fat, until the meat is browned and has taken on good grill marks, 8 to 10 minutes.

RECIPE CONTINUES »

FOR THE CUCUMBER YOGURT

1 cup plain **whole-milk Greek yogurt**

1 cup finely chopped **seedless cucumber**

2 tablespoons chopped **fresh dill**

2 teaspoons **fresh lemon juice**

Kosher salt and freshly ground **black pepper**

FOR SERVING

4 (6-inch) **whole wheat flat pitas**

2 cups finely shredded **romaine**

1 cup roughly chopped **tomato** (about 1 large beefsteak, or 2 to 4 plum), seeded

½ small **red onion**, thinly sliced

5. Flip the lamb over and cook until the lamb is medium rare, approximately another 8 to 10 minutes, depending on the heat of your grill and the thickness of your meat (a meat thermometer inserted into the center will read 125°F). Transfer the lamb to a cooling rack over a baking sheet and let rest for 5 minutes. Thinly slice across the grain of the meat and set aside.

6. Assemble the pitas: Warm the pitas on the grill, 10 to 15 seconds on each side. Pile the center of each pita with lamb slices and top with the carrot slaw, lettuce, tomato, and onion. Serve the cucumber yogurt on the side to drizzle on top.

NOTE: If you marinate your lamb overnight before cooking, wait until you're ready to eat before preparing your condiments. You want them all as fresh as possible. Use flat pitas, not pockets, for this recipe—they're thicker, softer, and less prone to breakage. And, if you don't have access to a gas or charcoal grill, a grill pan on the stovetop will do just fine.

BUTTERMILK FRIED CHICKEN AND WAFFLE SANDWICHES

Serves 4

While this is by no means a light dish (okay, it's a little over the top), it *is* a somewhat lighter take on a Southern restaurant favorite.

Wheat flour is the most common breading for "classic" American fried chicken. But across Asia, rice flour is often used instead. We take a tip from the East here, using only white rice flour to make the chicken's crust super crisp, rendered even more so by double-dipping the chicken into the batter.

1 tablespoon **Sriracha sauce**

½ cup **mayonnaise**

2 (6-ounce) **boneless, skinless chicken breasts**

1 cup **white rice flour**

2 teaspoons **garlic powder**

Heaping ½ teaspoon **smoked paprika**

Heaping ½ teaspoon **cayenne**

Heaping ½ teaspoon **kosher salt**

¼ teaspoon freshly ground **black pepper**

2 cups **buttermilk**

1 tablespoon **soy sauce** or **tamari**

Vegetable or **canola oil**, for frying

3 **Crispy Belgian Waffles** (½ recipe, page 68; see Note, page 147)

Quick-Pickled Vegetables (recipe follows)

1. Mix the Sriracha sauce and mayonnaise in a small bowl. Set aside.

2. Using a sharp knife, slice each chicken breast in half lengthwise. One at a time, put each half in a gallon-size plastic zippered bag. Using a meat mallet, rolling pin, or frying pan, pound the cutlet to ¼-inch thickness. Repeat with remaining cutlets.

3. Whisk together the rice flour, garlic powder, paprika, cayenne, salt, and pepper in a shallow baking dish. In a separate shallow baking dish or mixing bowl, mix the buttermilk and soy sauce.

4. Working one by one, dredge each chicken cutlet in the buttermilk mixture, allowing any excess to drip off. Next, dip them into the flour mixture, turning to coat it fully, then gently shake off any excess. Repeat, dipping the chicken in the buttermilk and then the flour mixture.

5. Preheat the oven to 200°F. Line a baking sheet with a couple layers of paper towels or a brown paper bag.

6. Pour the oil to a quarter-inch depth in a large skillet and heat over medium-high heat until the oil begins to shimmer and thins slightly. Using your fingers or tongs, gently lay 1 chicken cutlet in the oil. Cook, undisturbed, until the breading is a deep golden brown and crisp to the touch of the tongs, 3 minutes. Gently flip and cook on the opposite side, another 3 minutes. The crust should be dark brown, almost a deep caramel on the pointy crags where breading has collected. Remove the chicken from the pan with tongs to the lined baking sheet. To check for doneness, cut a slit in the thickest part of the chicken and make sure there is no pink left and the juices run clear. Keep warm in the oven while you cook the remaining 3 chicken cutlets, one at a time.

RECIPE CONTINUES ➻

7. When the chicken is cooked, make the waffles. As you finish cooking a waffle, keep it warm in the oven while you cook the remaining ones.

8. To serve, cut each waffle into quarters. (Belgian waffle makers draw the lines clearly for you.) For each sandwich, slather 1 quarter-segment of waffle generously with the Sriracha mayonnaise, then top with a fried chicken cutlet, heap with the pickled vegetables, and top with another waffle quarter. Serve immediately.

Quick-Pickled Vegetables

Makes 3 to 4 cups, depending on the size of the vegetables

Crunchy, tart, and sweet, these are a terrific counterpoint to rich meats in a sandwich. They're also terrific on their own, eaten straight from the container as a snack.

1 cup **rice wine vinegar**

2 tablespoons **sugar**

1 **jícama**, peeled

1 medium **carrot**

1 medium **zucchini**

1 medium **red onion**, sliced into thin half-moons

1 **red bell pepper**, seeded, cored, and julienned

¼ cup chopped **fresh cilantro**

Kosher salt and freshly ground **black pepper**

In a large bowl, combine the vinegar and sugar, stirring until the sugar dissolves. Using a mandoline with a julienne blade attached, cut up the jícama, carrot, and zucchini (if you're using a knife, thinly slice the vegetables before cutting them into long thin strips). Add the vegetables to the vinegar mixture along with the red onion and bell pepper. Add the cilantro, salt, and pepper to taste and toss. Cover and chill for at least 2 hours. (The vegetables stay crisp, covered in the refrigerator, for up to 1 week.)

NOTES: While our waffle recipe has plenty of gluten, if you use gluten-free tamari in your chicken, you have an entirely gluten-free fried chicken recipe here. Use it in sandwiches with gluten-free bread, slice and toss it over salads, or serve with a squeeze of lemon (or lime) alongside some crisp greens, as the Italians do alla Milanesa.

This recipe calls for a half batch of the waffles on page 68. We suggest you go ahead and make a whole batch of waffles and freeze the extras. But you can also prepare half a batch of batter and have just enough for this recipe.

147

FOR THE PEPPADEW SLAW

½ small head of **green cabbage** (see Note)

1 teaspoon **kosher salt**

¼ cup **mayonnaise**

1½ teaspoons **apple cider vinegar**

½ teaspoon freshly ground **black pepper**

5 **peppadews**, thinly sliced (about ⅓ cup)

FOR THE PORK

2 pounds **boneless pork loin** (see Note)

1 tablespoon **vegetable oil**

1 teaspoon **kosher salt**

1 teaspoon freshly ground **black pepper**

1 teaspoon **smoked paprika**

½ teaspoon **dried thyme**

FOR THE CHIPOTLE MAYONNAISE

2 canned **chipotle peppers in adobo**

¾ cup **mayonnaise**

4 **ciabatta rolls**, halved and toasted

ROAST PORK SANDWICHES
WITH PEPPADEW SLAW AND CHIPOTLE MAYONNAISE

Serves 4

This sandwich is sophisticated and a little edgy, like a leather jacket worn over a little black dress. Roast pork is amped up with a tangy peppadew-laced slaw and given extra heat from chipotles in adobo. Spicy and acidic, luscious and crunchy, deeply comforting but kind of out there: who says you can't have it all?

1. **Start the slaw:** Remove the tough outer leaves of the cabbage, then cut out the core. Thinly slice the cabbage and place it in a large bowl (you want about 2 cups, sliced). Sprinkle the salt over the top and mix thoroughly. Cover with plastic wrap and set in the fridge for at least 4 hours or overnight.

2. Position a rack in the center of the oven and preheat to 375°F.

3. **Roast the pork:** Place the meat in a large baking dish, fat side up. Drizzle the oil over the meat, then sprinkle evenly with the salt, pepper, paprika, and thyme. Roast until a bit browned and crusty on top and a meat thermometer stuck in the center reads 145°F, about 1 hour. Set aside to rest.

4. **Meanwhile, make the chipotle mayonnaise:** In the bowl of a food processor, combine the chipotles and mayonnaise. Whizz until it's a smooth ruddy paste, about 30 seconds (you may need to stop once or twice to scrape down the sides). Set aside.

5. **Finish the slaw:** Remove the cabbage from the fridge. Squeeze the cabbage to remove excess water and transfer to a clean large bowl. In a small bowl, combine the mayo, vinegar, and black pepper. Pour over the cabbage, and toss to combine. Add the peppadews and toss again. Set aside.

6. When the meat has rested at least 15 minutes, cut it against the grain into thin slices. Slather both halves of the ciabatta rolls with the chipotle mayonnaise, then layer on several slices of pork, and pile high with the slaw. Serve immediately.

NOTES: Salt the cabbage for your slaw at least 4 hours before mixing in the rest of the ingredients or, better yet, overnight. You'll draw moisture out of the cabbage and have much crunchier slaw as a result.

Don't be tempted to trim the fat off your pork loin here; it keeps the meat moist during roasting and helps crisp the outer layer. And per that outer layer, we keep the herb and salt crusting intact for serving, but if it's too intense for your liking, feel free to scrape off the spice mix after the meat has rested a bit, but before slicing.

KIMCHI-BULGOGI SANDWICHES

Serves 4

Bulgogi is Korean for "fire meat" or, translated, marinated meat (usually beef or pork) cooked on a grill. What sets it apart from workaday American grilled meats is its distinct marinade, a complex spicy-sweet slurry that, most critically, includes fresh fruit, which has enzymes to help tenderize the meat, and gochujang, a thick, fiery fermented paste made from chiles and glutinous brown rice. Here, we give flank steak the bulgogi treatment, then pile it high on chewy bread with kimchi (we use Kimchee Harvest in Roxbury) for funk and crunch, a sprinkle of fresh cilantro, and a slathering of cooling mayonnaise.

1. **Prepare the steak:** Combine the pear, garlic, onion, scallions, ginger, brown sugar, gochujang, soy sauce, and sesame oil in a blender and whizz until very smooth, stopping along the way to scrape down the sides with a rubber spatula. Place the steak in a medium bowl or large glass baking dish. Season both sides with the salt and pepper. Pour the marinade over the top, turn over to coat the other side, and jiggle around slightly to cover the steak completely with the marinade. Cover with plastic wrap and refrigerate at least 8 hours, or overnight.

2. Heat a grill or grill pan over high heat until smoking hot. Meanwhile, remove the meat from the marinade, holding the steak over the bowl to allow excess liquid to drip off (if the marinade is clinging to the meat in globs, gently scrape off the excess). Grill the steak for 4 to 5 minutes on each side for medium rare, then take it off the heat and allow to rest 10 minutes.

3. **Assemble the sandwiches:** Spread mayo on half of the bread. When the meat has rested, cut it into ¼-inch-thick slices. Divide the meat evenly across the bread, then do the same with the kimchi, cilantro, and sliced scallions. Top with the other half of the bread and serve.

NOTE: Gochujang is increasingly accessible in supermarkets, but if you can't find it at yours, it's widely available online.

FOR THE STEAK

1 ripe **pear** (any variety), peeled, cored, and cut into chunks (about 1 cup)

7 **garlic cloves**

1 medium **onion**, cut into large chunks (about 1 cup)

3 **scallions**, roughly chopped, plus more, thinly sliced, for garnish

2-inch piece of **fresh ginger**, peeled and roughly chopped

2 packed tablespoons **dark brown sugar**

½ cup **gochujang** (see Note)

¼ cup **soy sauce** or **tamari**

¼ cup **toasted sesame oil**

1½ pounds **flank steak**

2 teaspoons **kosher salt**

1 teaspoon freshly ground **black pepper**

FOR SERVING

¼ cup **mayonnaise**

1 fresh **baguette** or 4 **ciabatta rolls**, cut in half lengthwise and toasted

2 cups **kimchi**, drained and roughly chopped

¾ cup whole **fresh cilantro leaves**

HERB BUTTERMILK DRESSING

¼ cup **mayonnaise**

¼ cup **crème fraîche**

1 tablespoon **Dijon mustard**

¼ cup **buttermilk**

1 **garlic clove**, grated

1 small **shallot**, finely chopped (about 1 heaping tablespoon)

2 tablespoons finely chopped **fresh chives**

1 tablespoon finely chopped **fresh dill**

1 tablespoon finely chopped **fresh flat-leaf parsley**

1 teaspoon **kosher salt**

½ teaspoon freshly ground **black pepper**

FOR SERVING

4 **Kaiser rolls** or **brioche buns**, sliced and toasted

4 breaded and cooked **chicken cutlets** (from Buttermilk Fried Chicken and Waffle Sandwiches, page 145), hot

Bread and Butter Pickles (recipe follows)

8 slices ripe **tomato** (1 to 2 large)

3 cups shredded **romaine hearts** (from about 8 full leaves)

SPICY CHICKEN SANDWICHES
WITH BREAD AND BUTTER PICKLES
Serves 4

This is our version of the ubiquitous fried chicken sandwich found at fast-food joints: spicy, crunchy, and totally satisfying. While the sandwich comes together quickly once the component pieces are prepared, this meal involves a little forethought: you want your bread and butter pickles (recipe follows) to cure for at least three days before eating them. For extra spice, bump up the cayenne in the fried chicken or top with your favorite hot sauce.

1. **Make the dressing:** In a medium bowl, whisk together the mayonnaise, crème fraîche, mustard, buttermilk, garlic, and shallot. Add the herbs, salt, and pepper and stir gently to combine. (Ideally this dressing is prepared and used immediately, but it will keep for up to 2 days, covered, in the fridge.)

2. **Assemble the sandwiches:** Onto one half of each roll, layer 1 chicken cutlet, 5 to 10 pickle slices (depending on your penchant for brininess), 2 tomato slices, and 2 tablespoons of the dressing. Top with ¾ cup shredded romaine. Place the other half of the roll on top, and serve immediately.

RECIPE CONTINUES ➤

Bread and Butter Pickles

Makes 1 quart

1 large **English hothouse cucumber**, sliced ¼ inch thick
    (about 4 loosely packed cups; a mandoline is helpful here)

1 tablespoon **kosher salt**

2 cups **apple cider vinegar**

½ cup packed **dark brown sugar**

2-inch piece **fresh ginger**, peeled and roughly chopped

1 small **shallot**, roughly chopped (1 heaping tablespoon)

5 **garlic cloves**, smashed

1 tablespoon **ground turmeric**

1 tablespoon **yellow mustard seeds**

1 tablespoon **fennel seeds**

1 teaspoon **coriander seeds**

1 teaspoon **celery seeds**

3 **star anise**

1 tablespoon **black peppercorns**

1 **jalapeño pepper**, thinly sliced

1. Toss the cucumber with the salt in a medium bowl, cover, and let sit overnight, or for at least 8 hours, in the fridge. Pour the cucumber slices into a colander, draining off the liquid.

2. Combine the vinegar, 1 cup water, brown sugar, ginger, shallot, garlic, turmeric, mustard seeds, fennel seeds, coriander seeds, celery seeds, star anise, black peppercorns, and jalapeño in a medium saucepan. Over high heat, bring the mixture to a rolling boil. Turn off the heat and allow the mixture to steep for 1 hour.

3. Transfer the prepared cucumber slices to a quart-size glass canning jar or other heatproof container.

4. Pour the brine through a sieve into a medium bowl, then return the strained liquid to the saucepan. Return the brine to a boil, just for a moment, then carefully pour it over the cucumber slices. Stir gently to ensure the hot brine comes into contact with all the surface area of the cucumbers. Cover the container with its lid or plastic wrap, and allow the pickles to sit at room temperature for an hour, then move into the refrigerator. The pickles can be eaten 24 hours after preparing them, but for the fullest flavor, allow them to cure for at least 3 days. (They will keep in an airtight container in the fridge for up to 2 weeks.)

PORK BELLY BLTS
WITH BASIL AIOLI

Serves 4

Here's the number 1 rule with tomatoes: when you've got a really good one, leave it alone. We get plenty of good ones during high summer here in the Hudson Valley, which is the only time we serve this sandwich. Surrounded by farms, we get our tomatoes right after they've been picked—exactly how you want them.

In the classic BLT, the crispness of the lettuce, the mild creaminess of the mayo, and the salty crunch of the bacon all serve to elevate the perfection of a summer tomato. There's arguably no need to mess with a classic as good as a BLT, but playfulness is part of our style. This rendition ups the meat quotient, with thick, spicy cured pork belly in lieu of bacon (lending a toothsome chewiness in place of bacon's crumbly snap), and basil aioli providing a little more lusciousness than traditional mayo. You'll need to cure the pork belly a day ahead, so be sure to plan accordingly.

Cured Pork Belly
(page 83), chilled

8 slices **sourdough bread**, toasted

Basil Aioli
(recipe follows)

4 large leaves of crisp **lettuce** (such as romaine, Boston, or green leaf)

2 large ripe **tomatoes**, sliced

1. Slice the pork belly into ¼-inch-thick pieces, cut lengthwise so they're approximately the size of your toasted bread. Return the pork slices to the fridge for at least 10 minutes to fully chill.

2. Line a plate with paper towels. Heat a large sauté pan over medium-high heat and lay 5 or 6 pieces of pork belly into the pan. Cook until brown and crispy on both sides, 3 to 4 minutes per side. Carefully pour the fat from the pan into a glass or metal container, or directly into the trash.

Transfer the belly to the paper towel–lined plate, drain any remaining fat, and repeat the process with the remaining belly.

3. Spread the bread generously with the aioli. Divide the pork belly among the 4 sandwiches and top each with a lettuce leaf, several slices of tomato, and the remaining slices of bread. Serve immediately.

RECIPE CONTINUES ➺

Basil Aioli

Makes about 1 cup

Aioli is one of those recipes that can make novices nervous. Don't be. Just remember to work with best quality ingredients—no shriveled, year-old garlic or slightly rancid oil here. Make sure everything is fresh, fresh, fresh. And speaking of freshness, here's a reminder: aioli is made with raw egg yolks. We always recommend you be fastidious with your egg sourcing, but this is one application where you want to be particularly careful; a fresh egg from a really reliable source is your safest bet. If you're getting your eggs fresh from a farm, give them a wash under warm water with soap before cracking, as farm-fresh eggs often have bits of hay and other coop remnants clinging to their shells.

2 large **egg yolks**

2 **garlic cloves**, minced

2 tablespoons **fresh lemon juice**

2 teaspoons **Dijon mustard**

½ cup **grapeseed oil**

½ cup **olive oil**

Leaves from 1 small bunch **fresh basil**, finely chopped
   (about ¼ cup)

Kosher salt

1. In a small mixing bowl, combine the egg yolks, garlic, lemon juice, and mustard. Whisk together until smooth and creamy.

2. Combine the grapeseed oil and olive oil in a measuring cup. Slowly drizzle into the egg yolk mixture while whisking vigorously until all the oil is incorporated. If the aioli is too thick for your liking, adjust the consistency by adding warm water a few drops at a time while whisking.

3. Fold in the basil and season with salt. (The aioli will keep in the fridge for up to 3 days.)

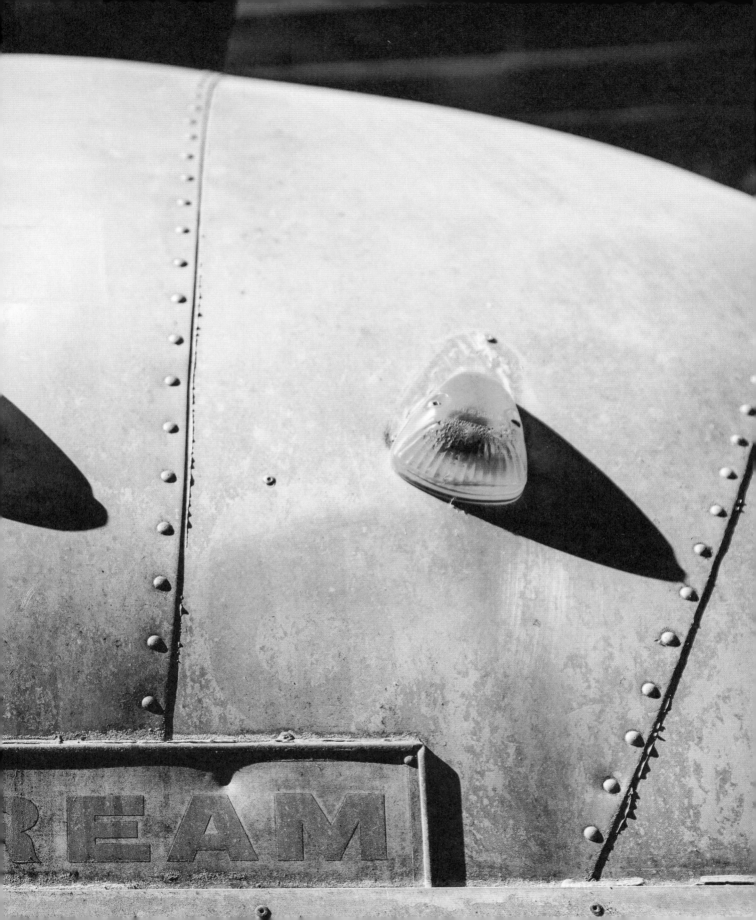

MEATBALL SLIDERS
WITH TOMATO, BASIL, AND MOZZARELLA
Serves 4

FOR THE TOMATO SAUCE

¼ cup **olive oil**

1 small **onion**, minced

3 **garlic cloves**, minced

½ cup **red wine**

1 (28-ounce) can crushed **tomatoes**

Kosher salt and freshly ground **black pepper**

FOR THE MEATBALLS

1 pound **ground beef** (80% lean)

½ pound **ground pork**

1 **shallot**, minced

3 **garlic cloves**, minced

1 large **egg**

½ cup **panko breadcrumbs**

¼ cup **whole milk**

¼ cup grated **parmesan cheese**

1 tablespoon chopped **fresh parsley**

2 teaspoons chopped **fresh oregano**

2 teaspoons **kosher salt**

2 teaspoons freshly ground **black pepper**

2 teaspoons **olive oil**

FOR SERVING

1 (8-ounce) ball of **fresh mozzarella**

12 **fresh basil leaves**

12 **slider buns**

Truth be told, we're mostly glad to see the era of ubiquitous sliders behind us. Not everything shines on a teeny, tiny bun. But these do. Carby, meaty, smothered in tomato sauce, and topped with melted cheese, these sliders are an homage in miniature to Mike's Italian American roots. They make a satisfying stand-alone meal and are classy enough to serve at a dinner party, but homey enough to share with your sweatpants-level friends.

The sauce recipe will make 1 quart—more than you need for this dish. Don't be tempted to halve it, as cooking tomato sauce in tiny batches causes it to thicken too fast. You also need the extra sauce to simmer the meatballs, so the flavors can meld. Use leftover sauce on pasta or spread onto crusty bread, top with fresh mozzarella, and slide under the broiler until the cheese is melting and bubbly for a quick snack.

1. Make the tomato sauce: In a large saucepan, heat the olive oil over medium heat. Add the onion and garlic and cook, stirring occasionally, until the onion and garlic are soft, about 5 minutes. Add the wine and increase the heat to high. Cook until all the liquid is evaporated, 3 to 5 minutes.

2. Add the crushed tomatoes and continue to cook over high heat until the sauce comes to a boil. Reduce the heat to low, season with salt and pepper, and simmer, uncovered, until the sauce has thickened slightly, is a deep red, and has turned less acidic, about 30 minutes.

3. Make the meatballs: In a large mixing bowl, combine the ground beef, ground pork, shallot, garlic, and egg and knead together with your hands until the mixture is smooth and slightly tacky.

4. In a medium bowl, combine the panko, milk, parmesan, parsley, oregano, salt, and pepper. Stir together until all the milk is absorbed, then add the mixture to the meat. Knead together until the breadcrumb mixture is fully absorbed and the meat is lighter and softer in texture. Place the mixture in the fridge to chill for at least 30 minutes.

5. Preheat the oven to 425°F. Grease a 9 by 13-inch baking dish with the olive oil.

6. Divide the meat into 12 equal balls, roughly 2 ounces in weight apiece (a standard ice cream scoop is a perfect measuring tool here). Using slightly damp hands, roll the meatballs in your cupped palms, pressing gently. Place the meatballs in the baking dish, making sure they don't touch one another so that they brown evenly in the oven. Bake until the meatballs are a deep brown color and firm to the touch, 20 to 25 minutes.

7. Remove the meatballs from the oven and carefully drain the fat from the pan. Carefully pour all the tomato sauce into the baking dish with the meatballs, and return to the oven. Cook until the sauce has begun to form a ruddy crust around the edges of the dish and the meatballs are easily pierced with a fork, an additional 10 minutes.

8. **Assemble the sliders:** Split the mozzarella ball in half lengthwise and cut each half into 6 slices. Remove the meatballs from the oven, top each ball with a basil leaf and a slice of mozzarella. Return the baking dish to the oven and cook until the cheese is soft and melted, about 5 minutes.

9. Place the slider buns on a baking sheet and slide them into the oven to warm for a minute. Use a slotted spoon to place a meatball and a small amount of sauce inside each bun. Serve immediately.

HEARTY MAINS AND SIDES

SALISBURY STEAK
WITH MUSHROOM GRAVY

Serves 4

2 pounds **ground beef**
(90% lean; see Note)

3 tablespoons **olive oil**

2 **shallots**, minced

3 **garlic cloves**,
minced

1 teaspoon chopped
fresh rosemary

1 teaspoon **fresh
thyme leaves**

½ cup **panko
breadcrumbs**

1 large **egg**

3 tablespoons
whole milk

3 tablespoons **tomato
ketchup**

3 tablespoons
Worcestershire sauce

1 tablespoon **Dijon
mustard**

2 tablespoons
kosher salt

1 teaspoon freshly
ground **black pepper**

1 tablespoon
vegetable oil

Mushroom Gravy
(page 132)

TV dinners are as all-American as diners. Chef Chris, for one, doesn't think they deserve the bad name they get. TV dinners were mainstays of the working mother of the 1970s and early '80s, part of our culture trying to adjust to changing norms in family life. He grew up on those frozen, compartmentalized meals. This version—a hamburger steak smothered in mushroom gravy—was a favorite of his, and is an homage to those filling staples of weekday evening freedom; all that's missing is the brownie baked into the little aluminum tray.

This recipe makes four ample patties that cook up super moist and tender, each one a hearty main course. Serve with Garlic Mashed Potatoes (page 195) and sautéed Wax Beans and Fennel with Dill (page 200), or simply alongside a green salad. The steaks keep well in the fridge as well—use leftovers like you would meatloaf. They're especially good sandwiched between slices of crusty bread as a take-along lunch.

1. Preheat the oven to 375°F. Place the ground beef in a large bowl and place in the refrigerator to thoroughly chill while preparing the other ingredients.

2. In a medium sauté pan, heat the olive oil over medium heat. Add the minced shallots and garlic and cook, stirring occasionally, until soft and translucent, 5 minutes. Stir in the rosemary, thyme, and panko, then remove the pan from the heat and let cool to room temperature.

3. In a small bowl, whisk together the egg, milk, ketchup, Worcestershire sauce, and mustard.

4. Remove the ground beef from the fridge and add the shallot and egg mixtures. Season with the salt and pepper and mix thoroughly.

5. Divide the meat into 4 equal portions. Roll into a ball and then press into a flat oval roughly ¾ inch thick. The mixture is going to feel pretty wet at this point, but don't fear; as with biscuits and gnocchi, where the dough is meant to be wet, use a light touch and have a little faith! You'll be rewarded with a fabulously tender and moist end product.

6. Heat a large ovenproof sauté pan (13-inch will fit all 4, but know it'll be tight!) over medium-high heat and add the vegetable oil. When the oil is hot, shimmering, and just starts to smoke, carefully add the patties one at a time. Cook until the steak is dark brown but not black, 2 to 3 minutes per side (the steak will finish cooking in the oven).

7. Add the mushroom gravy to the pan, smothering the steaks as you go, then place the pan in the oven and bake until the beef is fully cooked (the internal temperature will be 140°F), 8 to 10 minutes.

8. To serve, dish up one steak and one-fourth of the gravy onto each plate (you'll have a very healthy portion of gravy, "smothering" the steak).

NOTE: For this recipe, you'll want to use a fairly lean ground beef mixture. Look for no less than 90% lean, as these patties give off a fair bit of fat as they cook in the skillet. And though it might seem redundant to put your beef back into the fridge, it's not. You want your beef to be *really* cold, allowing the fat to emulsify when you start mixing it instead of just separating out on its own.

BAKED POLENTA
WITH KALE AND PUMPKIN
Serves 4 to 6

This is a hearty baked dish perfect for chilly weather. It feels virtuous, with plenty of vegetables, but it isn't the least bit austere. Here, we give our Classic Cheddar Grits (page 53) a little makeover, substituting polenta for the stone-ground grits and fresh goat cheese for the cheddar. This lends lusciousness and a little tang to cut through the rich, mellow flavor of the roasted pumpkin. Speaking of which, we use an heirloom Cinderella pumpkin, which is earthy and has dense flesh that holds up well in a hot oven. Look for pumpkins labeled "pie" or "sugar." If you're unable to find cooking pumpkins, butternut squash will do just fine.

This dish makes a lovely lunch or dinner and works nicely as a brunch dish, as well. Leftovers, cut into squares, warmed in the oven, and topped with a fried egg, make a terrific and quick breakfast.

A reminder: the polenta is a long affair. Make sure you allow adequate cooking time.

1 cup **polenta** (we use Wild Hive)

2 cups **whole milk**, plus more as needed

1 teaspoon **fine sea salt**

1½ cups (12 ounces) **fresh goat cheese**

3 tablespoons **unsalted butter**

Freshly ground **black pepper**

2 tablespoons **olive oil**

3 cups cubed (about ½ inch) **pumpkin**

Kosher salt

1 bunch of **lacinato (dinosaur) kale**, stemmed and roughly chopped (6 to 8 loosely packed cups)

½ cup grated **parmesan cheese**

1. In a heavy-bottomed pot, combine the polenta and 2 cups water, and gently stir a few times with a wooden spoon. Skim off any bits of hull or chaff that float to the top, then cover and leave to soak at room temperature at least 8 hours, or overnight.

2. In the morning, add the milk to the pot and cook over medium-high heat, stirring constantly to keep the milk and polenta from sticking to the bottom, until the polenta begins to thicken and bubble, 7 to 10 minutes. Reduce the heat to the lowest setting possible and cover. Cook, uncovering only to stir every 20 minutes or so, until the polenta appears smooth and creamy, but fairly firm. This can take anywhere from 30 minutes to 1 hour, depending on what "low" is like on your range, and whether you're

working over gas or electric heat. If the polenta seems a bit dry (chunky rather than lusciously smooth), add as much as another ½ cup milk, in 2-tablespoon increments, and cook for another 10 to 15 minutes, until the grits have smoothed and absorbed all the additional liquid.

3. When the polenta is fully cooked and at the right consistency, add the sea salt, 8 ounces (1 cup) of the goat cheese, and 1 tablespoon of the butter, and stir until incorporated. Remove from the heat and top with a few turns from a pepper mill.

4. Preheat the oven to 375°F. Grease an 8-inch square baking dish with the remaining 2 tablespoons butter, then pour in the polenta. Set aside while you work on the vegetables.

RECIPE CONTINUES ➦

5. Heat a medium skillet over high heat. Add the olive oil, and when it begins to shimmer, add the pumpkin and sprinkle lightly with kosher salt and a few twists of the pepper mill. Cook, stirring only occasionally to prevent burning, until the pumpkin has caramelized slightly but is still firm and holding its shape, 7 to 8 minutes. Add the kale and about 2 tablespoons water, along with another pinch of salt. Give a quick stir, then cover with a lid for 3 minutes in order to steam the vegetables a bit; the kale will be slightly wilted, and will have turned a brighter green.

6. Pour the vegetables over the top of the polenta, and spread evenly. Pinch marble-sized blobs of the remaining goat cheese and scatter them across the surface of the vegetables, then sprinkle the parmesan over the top. Bake until the cheese has slightly browned and formed a crust over the top, about 20 minutes. The polenta will have become very loose, almost soupy. Set aside on a heatproof surface to allow the polenta to set slightly and cool, about 20 minutes. Serve family style or spoon out into deep bowls.

CHILE-BRAISED LAMB TOSTADAS

Serves 4

Open-faced sandwiches have long been featured as blue plate specials, but tostadas—their south-of-the-border cousins—are far less common on diner menus. We're advocates of their widespread adoption: crispy fried corn tortillas make a lighter (and gluten-free) alternative to thick slices of bread and are better suited to big piles of fresh vegetables that you don't want to go soggy. Tostadas are a blank slate and can take on almost any combination of ingredients and flavors. This one marries the Mexican roots of many of our kitchen staff with the prevalence of lamb in Greek cuisine (a.k.a. classic American diner).

1. **Make the lamb:** In a Dutch oven or other large heavy-bottomed pot with a lid, heat the oil over high heat until it just begins to smoke. Add the lamb and cook, stirring occasionally, until well browned, about 10 minutes. Once it's browned, season lightly with salt and pepper. Add the salsa, chicken broth, and orange juice and bring to a boil. Reduce the heat to low and cover, cooking undisturbed, until the lamb is very tender and begins to fall apart, about 2 hours. Set aside for about half an hour to cool. Use a slotted spoon to transfer the meat from the pot to a plate, discarding the cooking liquid.

2. **Prepare the tostadas:** Set a large heavy skillet over medium-high heat and add the vegetable oil to a ½-inch depth. Heat until a candy thermometer reads 375°F. While the oil is heating, poke the tortillas all over with the tip of a sharp knife. Line a large plate or baking sheet with paper towels.

3. When the oil is hot, working one by one, use tongs to gently lay a tortilla into the oil, cooking until puffed, crispy, and lightly golden brown, about 15 seconds per side. Transfer the tortilla to the paper towel–lined plate and season lightly with salt. Repeat with the remaining tortillas.

4. **Assemble the tostadas:** Spread about ¼ cup of the refried beans on each tostada. Layer on a mound of lamb, romaine, tomatoes, red onion, and avocado. Drizzle with crema and top with cilantro. Dig in immediately.

NOTES: Get going on your beans the day before. If you like, you can braise the lamb then, too; simply store it, covered, in the fridge, then warm it in a saucepan set over very low heat when you're getting ready to eat. All that'll be left to do is to prepare your toppings, fry the tortillas, and assemble.

  If you can't find Mexican crema, sour cream will work fine. Just pull it out of the fridge at least 30 minutes before you're ready to assemble the tostadas so it loosens up a bit.

RECIPE CONTINUES ➺

FOR THE LAMB

¼ cup **vegetable oil**

1 pound **boneless lamb shoulder or leg**, cut into 1-inch cubes (see Note)

Kosher salt and freshly ground **black pepper**

1¾ cups **Salsa Roja** (½ recipe; page 51)

1 cup **low-sodium chicken broth**

1 cup **orange juice**

FOR THE TOSTADAS

Vegetable oil, for frying

4 **corn tortillas**

Kosher salt

FOR SERVING

1 cup **Refried Pinto Beans**, warmed (recipe follows)

1 **romaine heart**, shredded

1 pint **cherry tomatoes**, halved

1 small **red onion**, sliced into thin half-moons

1 ripe **avocado**, sliced

½ cup **Mexican crema** (see Note)

¼ cup chopped **fresh cilantro**

HEARTY MAINS AND SIDES

171

Refried Pinto Beans

Makes about 6 cups

This recipe makes more refried beans than you'll need for the four tostadas, but they're so tasty and versatile that it's well worth making a big batch every time you cook them. Refried beans keep in an airtight container in the fridge for three or four days, or frozen for months. If you've frozen them, thaw in the fridge overnight, then gently warm in a saucepan with a little vegetable oil, adding a few tablespoons of water if needed to loosen the beans to a creamy, spreadable consistency.

1 pound **dried pinto beans**

¼ cup **vegetable oil**

1 large **onion**, minced (about 2 cups)

5 **garlic cloves**, minced

Kosher salt and freshly ground **black pepper**

1. Place the beans in a large bowl and pick through, removing any small stones or debris. Then add enough water to cover. Soak at least 6 hours, or overnight.

2. Drain the beans and put them in a large pot with enough water to cover by at least 3 inches. Bring to a boil over high heat, then reduce the heat to medium and cook, uncovered, until the beans are very soft, creamy, and beginning to fall apart, about 1 hour and 15 minutes. Let sit for about 30 minutes to cool in their cooking liquid.

3. Drain the beans into a colander set over a large bowl. Reserve 4 cups of the cooking liquid and discard the rest.

4. In a large saucepan, heat the oil over high heat until it shimmers. Add the onion and garlic and season lightly with salt and pepper. Cook, stirring occasionally, until the onion is translucent, about 5 minutes. Add the beans to the pot, along with 1¾ cups of the cooking liquid, and bring to a boil. Continue to cook on high heat (the beans will be bubbling vigorously) until the beans are falling apart and the mixture has begun to thicken, 5 to 10 minutes. Turn off the heat and allow to cool slightly.

5. Using a potato masher, smash the beans into a still chunky but thick and creamy paste, adding more cooking liquid as needed, 2 tablespoons at a time.

CHICKEN
WITH CHIVE-BUTTERMILK DUMPLINGS
Serves 6

This makes for a thick, chunky, hearty stew—real country food. Chicken and dumplings varies depending on the cook, and this is Chef Chris's version—filling yet delicate, full of vegetables and flavorful chunks of meat. But the real standout here is the dumplings, which are mini chive-flecked buttermilk biscuits that take the place of more traditional dropped-in dumplings. This dish would traditionally be thickened with flour, but Chris prefers cornstarch—it yields results that are silkier and less gummy. It may seem like quite a lot of cornstarch, but you're aiming for a stew with some backbone (it should hold its shape on the spoon) that offers a counterpoint to the buttery, flaky biscuits.

Traditionally, dumplings were added to stews as a cheap way to stretch whatever meat and vegetables were available to feed large families. The proportions here are in that spirit; this recipe may make more dumplings than you'd like to add to your stew. If so, store them in an airtight container overnight, reheat in a low (250°F) oven for a few minutes the next morning, and enjoy them with coffee and eggs for breakfast.

Follow the instructions in the order written here if you plan to do everything in a single day. But if you prefer, you can make the biscuits a day ahead; just store them in an airtight container until ready to add to the stew. And any butcher worth his or her salt should cut up a chicken for you if you ask nicely.

. . . .

1. Season the chicken pieces lightly with salt and pepper.

2. In a large Dutch oven, heat the oil over medium-high heat. Add the chicken, skin side down, and cook until well browned, 7 to 10 minutes. Flip the chicken pieces and cook until browned on the other side, an additional 5 to 7 minutes. Remove the chicken from the pot and discard the fat.

3. Return the chicken to the pot and cover with the stock. Add the thyme, rosemary, and bay leaves. Bring to a boil over high heat, then reduce the heat to low. Cover the pot and poach the chicken until just cooked through but still firm, 25 to 30 minutes. Turn off the heat, remove the lid, and let cool for 1 hour.

1 whole chicken (about 3 pounds), cut into 8 pieces (reserving the neck, back, and wings for stock)

Kosher salt and freshly ground **black pepper**

2 tablespoons **vegetable oil**

3 quarts homemade **chicken stock** (or canned low-sodium broth)

1 sprig of **fresh thyme**

1 sprig of **fresh rosemary**

2 **bay leaves**

1 large **onion**, coarsely chopped

2 medium **carrots**, cut into small cubes

3 **celery stalks**, cut into small cubes

2 **parsnips**, peeled and cut into small cubes

1 large **celery root**, peeled and cut into small cubes

½ cup **cornstarch**

1 cup **heavy cream**

Chive-Buttermilk Dumplings (recipe follows)

2 tablespoons chopped **fresh parsley**

RECIPE CONTINUES ➻

4. Transfer the chicken to a platter and discard the thyme, rosemary, and bay leaves. When cool enough to handle, pull the meat from the bones into large bite-size pieces. Discard the bones and skin.

5. Add the onion, carrots, celery, parsnips, and celery root to the broth and bring to a boil over high heat. Reduce the heat to medium and cook until the vegetables are just barely tender, 8 to 10 minutes.

6. In a liquid measuring cup, combine the cornstarch and cream. Use a fork to whisk until fully combined. Bring the broth back to a boil over high heat. Slowly pour in the cornstarch slurry while rapidly whisking. Allow the liquid to boil for 1 more minute while gently stirring to prevent the bottom from scorching.

7. Reduce the heat to medium-low and gently stir in the chicken meat and the dumplings. Simmer until the chicken is warm and the dumplings have barely softened but are still very much intact.

8. To serve, divide the stew among 6 large bowls and garnish with a generous sprinkling of parsley.

Chive-Buttermilk Dumplings

Makes 35 to 40 mini biscuits

2 cups **all-purpose flour**, plus more for dusting

2 tablespoons plus 1 teaspoon **baking powder**

1 teaspoon **baking soda**

2 teaspoons **kosher salt**

1 teaspoon freshly ground **black pepper**

6 tablespoons **unsalted butter**, frozen

1 cup **buttermilk**, chilled and shaken

¼ cup chopped **fresh chives**

1. Position a rack in the center of the oven and preheat the oven to 400°F.

2. Into a large bowl, sift together the flour, baking powder, baking soda, salt, and pepper. Set a box grater directly into the flour mixture, its base resting in the flour. Working quickly and using the largest holes of the grater, grate the frozen butter into the flour. Use your hands to gently knead the butter into the flour, just until it takes on the texture of coarse crumbs.

3. Make a well in the center of the mixture. Add the buttermilk and chives to the well and use a wooden spoon to pull scoops of flour into the buttermilk until the dough just comes together (don't be tempted to do any extra mixing, as you don't want to overwork the dough). Continue until all the flour has been incorporated (the dough should be a bit wet, but not too sticky). Press the dough together into a rough uneven ball, dipping your hands in flour if you find the dough is sticking to your skin.

4. Generously dust a work surface with flour. Turn the dough out and press it into a roughly rectangular shape about ½ inch thick. Brush off any excess flour from the top of the dough, then gently fold it in half and flatten again into the same shape and size.

5. Use a 1½-inch round biscuit cutter to cut the biscuits, leaving at least ⅛ inch between each cut. (Be sure to press the cutter straight down into the dough, as twisting will pinch the edges of the biscuits and prevent them from properly rising. Wipe the cutter clean and dip it into flour after every few cuts.) When you're done, you'll have between 35 and 40 mini biscuits.

6. Place the biscuits on an unlined baking sheet and bake until they're golden brown, 7 to 9 minutes. Set aside to cool.

Fly Fishing and the Fate of the Esopus Creek

The year was 1955, and her name was Old Bess. It was April 29 and the weather was verging on warm, but the wind howled and the rain came down in torrents in Phoenicia, New York. Larry Decker stood in the Esopus Creek, waiting, waiting. Suddenly, he had her on the end of the line. Commotion erupted. People arrived by car and foot, crowding around Decker. When, finally, he held her, mouth agape, her glory was evident to all those who had come: at 9½ pounds and 30¾ inches long, she was the largest brown trout ever caught in the Esopus.

Record-setting makes for a good story, but trout fishing has been a workaday part of Catskills life since long before European settlers made their way to the region. In Sullivan County, the Lenape Indians developed a way to attract the area's abundant trout using the bark of a walnut tree, a trick that effectively lured the fish to their demise. Due northeast, in Ulster County, the Algonquin tribe made their home along one of the main tributaries carrying water from the streams of the Catskills down to the Hudson River. When the Dutch came to the region, in the early 1600s, they named the creek Esopus, which was their mangled version of the Algonquin name for "small brook." The name stuck.

In the early nineteenth century, European settlers pushed deep into the dense hemlock forests of the Catskill hills and discovered the riches of the mountain streams. Early Hudson River School painters began carrying rods with them on their wilderness adventures, delighted by the bushels of brook trout they were able to catch. By 1830, Shandaken, New York, became home to Milo Barber, the first known fisherman's boardinghouse in America. Our region's famed nature writer, John Burroughs, wrote, "The water of all this Catskills region is the best in the world. . . . Trout streams gurgled about my family tree."

As the use of the area's brooks for sport grew, so did the fight for seclusion and wilderness resources. In the 1880s, New York State passed the club corporation law, which enabled sporting groups to buy up stretches of river frontage for private use, which, while exclusive, helped keep the streams uncrowded. The Great Trout War was waged as wealthy anglers hired game wardens to guard their river mileage against poachers.

But at the turn of the century, when the Catskills region was tapped as part of the watershed for the rapidly growing New York City, the area's fishing culture nearly ended for good. In 1906, construction of the Ashokan Reservoir began, signaling a major threat to the winding tributaries, and the fish, of the eastern Catskills. Meanwhile, the rise in sporting tourism had brought about overhunting, including the near extinction of turkeys, the disappearance of deer west of the Hudson by 1875, and the necessity of trout restocking in the area's streams and creeks in the 1870s. The wilderness shrank alongside the area's wildlife: by the 1880s, less than 25 percent of New York State was forested (today, that figure has risen to 63 percent).

The nascent fishing clubs came together in resistance. On January 13, 1923, the *Kingston Daily Freeman* announced the formation of Phoenicia Fish and Game, Inc., an organization whose intent was to sustain and preserve fish and game. They counted the fishing legend Ray Smith—the fly-tying innovator who led expeditions for the New York City branch of Abercrombie & Fitch and guided the likes of Fred Allen and Babe Ruth—among their own. The glue that held them together was a fierce devotion to protecting the wild character and lifestyle of the Catskills.

As more rivers were dammed in order to help quench New York City's seemingly insatiable thirst, the Esopus was bombarded with muddy, silt-laden water, with fluctuations in temperature and volume, and with new, warmer-water fish species. The clubs rose up in protest, winning a series of victories to regulate water flow into the region's waterways. In the 1970s and '80s, as the environmental movement in the United States gained ground, the group won two major battles against the state, one in favor of incremental water shutoffs and another against a pumped storage project proposed by the New York Power Authority.

Ashokan Reservoir (*Ashokan* means "place of fish"), still a major water supplier for New York City, has become a hub of recreation. A footpath crosses the stunning basin, water cupped in the bowl of the hills, and the reservoir has become a major fishing destination in its own right, annually stocked with brown trout to supplement the brown and rainbow trout that move between the Ashokan and the Upper Esopus in their annual spawning migration. In large part, it was the love of trout that saved this area's living waterways from ruin.

ESOPUS TROUT AND CHIPS

Serves 4

In our neck of the Catskills, the Esopus Creek is a favorite spot for swimming, tubing, camping, and rock clambering, but most of all the creek is synonymous with trout. For centuries, it has been one of *the* places to come to pluck your still-wriggling dinner from the stream. On any reasonably temperate day, you'll spot wader-clad folks in thigh-high waters at eddies, drop-offs, undercut banks, merging currents, and outside bends, gracefully casting their lines or awaiting bites.

The Phoenicia Diner sits just a stone's throw from the Esopus, and trout is featured all over our menu—smoked, roasted, and, most popular, fried. Here, we dredge delicate fillets in cornmeal and cook them up in a hot skillet, a quintessentially American mountain dish.

If you're catching your own fish, you're probably well versed in filleting. If you're buying your fish, ask the monger to fillet it for you and then do the portioning yourself. Or, if you're game, try to teach yourself basic filleting. It's an easy skill to acquire, and trout is one of the simplest fish on which to learn. The more often you fillet your fish, the more confident you'll become.

Serve the fried trout hot, alongside coleslaw (page 201) and fries, or "chips" (page 202) as a platter. Alternatively, serve the fish as sandwiches, heaping the trout on your bun of choice, topping it with coleslaw and bread and butter pickles (page 156).

Vegetable oil, for frying

2 rainbow trout (12 to 14 ounces each), filleted

2 cups buttermilk

3 cups fine cornmeal

1 tablespoon smoked paprika

1 tablespoon kosher salt

2 teaspoons freshly ground black pepper

Classic Coleslaw (page 201)

Phoenicia Diner French Fries (page 202)

Lemon wedges, for serving

1. Place a cast-iron skillet over high heat and fill with about ¼ inch of vegetable oil. Heat the oil to 375°F.

2. Cut each fish fillet crosswise into 3 equal pieces. Pour the buttermilk into a large shallow bowl and soak the trout pieces, fully submerged, in the buttermilk for 5 minutes. Meanwhile, in a medium bowl, mix the cornmeal, paprika, salt, and pepper.

3. Set up a breading station as close to your stove as possible, setting the cornmeal mixture next to the skillet and the buttermilk-soaked trout right beside the cornmeal. Line a plate with paper towels and set it aside.

4. Working one by one, allow the excess buttermilk to drop off the trout pieces, then place the fish in the cornmeal mixture, shaking the bowl gently to ensure that the trout is completely coated. Repeat until all the fish pieces are in the cornmeal mixture.

RECIPE CONTINUES ➤➤

5. Gently shake any excess coating from the trout pieces and lay them gently, one by one, in the skillet, being careful not to spatter yourself with hot oil. (You'll need to work in at least 2 batches here, making sure the fish pieces don't overlap with one another in the skillet.) Fry the trout pieces until light golden brown, about 2 minutes per side.

6. Transfer the fish to the paper towel–lined plate and season with salt. Repeat until all the trout pieces are fried. (You can keep the fried trout warm in a 200°F oven until all the fish has been cooked.)

7. Serve the fish hot with coleslaw, fries, and lemon wedges on the side.

MINI HERBED MEATLOAVES

Serves 6

In addition to proper seasoning, a good panade—simply a mixture of milk and dry bread (usually stale bread or breadcrumbs)—is the key to good meatloaf. The wet bread mixture helps thicken the meatloaf mixture while keeping the meat tender and moist during baking. We prefer dried herbs in sausages, meatloaf, meatballs, and the like—the flavor is punchier and seasons the meat more consistently throughout.

A couple of tips to save your meatloaf before it's too late: Crack your eggs into a separate bowl before adding them to the meat mixture. By that point in the process, you've put a lot of your ingredients (including meat, which doesn't come cheap) into a single mixing bowl. This is not the moment you want to discover you've got a bad egg and have to toss everything and start again.

If you're trying to get a jump on dinner, you can form these meatloaves the night or morning before you plan to eat them. Just cover the shaped loaves loosely with plastic wrap and refrigerate until you're a little over an hour from mealtime. Make sure you allow time to fully preheat your oven before baking the loaves.

Serve with a side of your choice, such as wax beans (page 200), mashed potatoes (page 195), or honey-glazed carrots (page 194).

¼ cup **olive oil**

1 medium **onion**, finely chopped (about 1 cup)

5 **garlic cloves**, minced

1 tablespoon **kosher salt**

2 teaspoons freshly ground **black pepper**

1 teaspoon **dried thyme**

1 teaspoon **dried oregano**

1 teaspoon **dried rosemary**

½ cup **whole milk**

1 cup **panko breadcrumbs**

2 large **eggs**

½ pound **ground pork**

1½ pounds **ground beef** (80% lean)

2 tablespoons **Worcestershire sauce**

½ cup **tomato ketchup**

1 tablespoon **Dijon mustard**

1. In a large skillet, warm the olive oil over medium heat. Add the onion and garlic, then season with the salt, pepper, thyme, oregano, and rosemary. Reduce the heat down to medium-low, and give everything a stir. Continue cooking, stirring occasionally to keep the onion from browning, until the onion is soft and translucent, 5 to 8 minutes. Remove the pan from the heat and let cool for at least 5 minutes.

2. In a large mixing bowl, combine the milk, panko, cooled onion (set the oily skillet aside; you'll need it again), and eggs and stir together. The mixture will be the texture of loose cornbread batter—this is your panade.

3. To the milk-panko mixture, add the pork and beef and combine using your hands or a wooden spoon. Add the Worcestershire sauce, ketchup, and mustard and continue mixing, working along the sides of the bowl to fold the meat over itself and back into the mixture, until thoroughly combined. The mixture will be loose and quite wet but will hold its shape in the bowl.

RECIPE CONTINUES ➸

4. Reheat the skillet over high heat. When a droplet of water sizzles and disappears, it's hot enough for cooking. Pat a large pinch (about 1 tablespoon) of the meatloaf mixture into a small patty (this is a mini tester patty) and lay it in the pan, cooking until brown and crusty, 1 or 2 minutes per side. Taste the meatloaf for seasoning, adding more salt as needed.

5. Line a rimmed baking sheet or a 9 by 13-inch baking dish with aluminum foil.

6. Divide the meat into 6 equal portions (about a heaping ¾ cup each). Using damp hands, pat each portion into an oval about 2 inches thick and 4 inches wide, pressing down gently on the top to make the shape of a small slightly deflated football. Lay the meatloaf on the foil-lined baking sheet. Repeat with the remaining meat until you have 6 small loaves, spacing them evenly across the pan. (If you find yourself with a bit of extra meat, make one more loaf.)

Slide the baking sheet into the fridge and chill, uncovered, for at least 20 minutes, or overnight. (You want the meat to be cold when it goes into the oven so that it retains more of its moisture.)

7. While the meatloaves are chilling, position the rack in the center of the oven and preheat the oven to 350°F.

8. Remove the pan with the loaves from the fridge and slide it directly into the oven. Bake for 20 minutes, then rotate 180 degrees and cook until the loaves bounce back to a gentle touch and have become russetty brown on top and deeper brown around the bases (where the loaves will have given off some fat), about 25 minutes. Remove the loaves from the oven and let them cool on their baking sheet. (The meatloaf will continue to cook a bit as it sits; don't be tempted to continue cooking in the oven.) Let rest 10 to 15 minutes on the baking sheet so the loaves can firm up a bit before serving.

SKIRT STEAK
WITH BALSAMIC ONIONS
Serves 4

This is summer food—simple, straightforward, the sort of thing you cook when you're planning a weekend away and don't want to pack all the ingredients and paraphernalia for a complicated meal. Lucky for us, you can find most of what you need for this dish at any of the roadside stands that dot the Catskills. Serve with Roasted High-Season Corn (page 197) and Summer's Bliss New Potatoes (page 196), both of which feature produce that appear in high summer. Eat this outside on a balmy evening, when the crickets are chirping and the days are still long. It's one of the best ways to savor the season.

1. Position a rack at the lowest setting and preheat the oven to 400°F.

2. **Make the balsamic onions:** Spread the onions in a 9 by 13-inch baking dish. In a small bowl, stir together the vinegar, olive oil, brown sugar, thyme, rosemary, salt, pepper, and garlic. Spoon the vinegar mixture over the top of the onions and cover the baking dish tightly with aluminum foil. Roast the onions until they've softened but still hold together, 25 to 30 minutes.

3. When the onions are done, carefully remove the foil. Add about 2 tablespoons water and give the pan a good shake. Then return the onions to the oven—this time uncovered—and cook for another 5 minutes. They will be glossy and have softened a bit, and the layers will have pulled apart some. Set the onions aside.

4. Heat a grill or a grill pan over high heat.

5. **Prepare the steak:** Season the meat well with salt and pepper. Cook the steaks for 3 minutes, undisturbed, then flip, cooking 3 more minutes on the other side for medium rare; the steaks will have deep charred grill marks. Using tongs or a fork, pull the steaks from the heat, set on a platter, and let rest.

6. By now, the onions will have released some liquid. Give all the contents of the baking dish a good stir. Top the slices of steak with the onions and some of their pan juices, and serve.

FOR THE BALSAMIC ONIONS

2 large **red onions**, each cut into 8 half-moon wedges

¼ cup **balsamic vinegar**

¼ cup **olive oil**

1 packed tablespoon **dark brown sugar**

1 teaspoon finely chopped **fresh thyme**

1 teaspoon finely chopped **fresh rosemary**

1 teaspoon **kosher salt**

½ teaspoon freshly ground **black pepper**

1 **garlic clove**, grated

FOR THE STEAK

1½ pounds **skirt steak**, divided into 4 (6-ounce) portions

Kosher salt and freshly ground **black pepper**

HERB AND LEMON ROAST CHICKEN

Serves 4

1 whole **chicken** (3 to 4 pounds)

1 tablespoon **kosher salt**

1 **lemon**, halved

1 sprig of **fresh rosemary**

3 sprigs of **fresh thyme**

3 **garlic cloves**, smashed

1 tablespoon **olive oil**

Freshly ground **black pepper**

At one time, comforting meat, starch, and vegetable plates—anchored by things like a perfect roast chicken—were the mainstay of diners. Sadly, this old-timey, no-frills kind of meal has gone out of fashion in restaurants. But we know our guests crave the same sorts of homey meals we do, so we've always featured old-school platters like this one on our menu.

The key to the best roast chicken is to salt ahead of time. The dry brine serves to season the bird and draw out excess moisture, which helps the skin become extra crispy during roasting. Serve this with Garlic Mashed Potatoes (page 195) and Honey-Glazed Carrots with Tarragon (page 194).

1. The day before you plan to cook your chicken, season the bird with salt all over the outside and in the cavity. Place on a plate and refrigerate, uncovered, at least 12 hours and up to 24 hours.

2. When you're ready to cook, position a rack in the center of the oven and preheat the oven to 450°F. Line a baking sheet with aluminum foil and place the chicken on it, breast side up.

3. Stuff the lemon halves, rosemary and thyme sprigs, and garlic into the cavity of the bird. Use butcher twine to truss the legs, pulling the thighs in tight to the bird and crossing the tips of the drumsticks in an X-shape to cover the opening of the cavity. Drizzle all over with olive oil and season with a few turns of the pepper mill.

4. Roast the chicken until the skin has begun to turn golden, 20 to 25 minutes. Then reduce the heat to 375°F and cook until the skin is golden brown all over, the drumstick is easy to jiggle, and when a knife is inserted through the thigh into the hip joint, the juices run clear, about another hour.

5. Pull the chicken from the oven and let rest 30 minutes before carving. Carve and serve.

HONEY-GLAZED CARROTS
WITH TARRAGON

Serves 4 as a side

2 tablespoons **olive oil**

1 generous pound **carrots** (4 to 6 fat storage carrots, or 6 to 8 thinner summer carrots), peeled and cut into ¼-inch rounds

Kosher salt and freshly ground **black pepper**

2 tablespoons **honey** (we use a wildflower varietal for this recipe)

1 tablespoon **fresh lemon juice**

1 tablespoon **unsalted butter**

1 tablespoon finely chopped **fresh tarragon**

These carrots are far less sweet than some glazed carrots you'll find on restaurant menus, with just a touch of honey amplifying the carrots' natural earthiness. The tarragon adds brightness, keeping the dish from feeling too wintry.

1. Set a large sauté pan over high heat. Add the olive oil, and when it begins to smoke, add the carrots. Season generously with salt and a few turns of the pepper mill, and cook, stirring occasionally, until they're still firm but have taken on some brown color, about 7 minutes. Reduce the heat to medium, and add the honey and lemon juice.

2. Cook until the liquid in the bottom of the pan has evaporated and the carrots are glossy with glaze, another 3 to 5 minutes. Turn off the heat, add the butter, and swirl the pan until the butter fully melts. Stir in the tarragon and serve.

GARLIC MASHED POTATOES

Serves 4 as a side

This is a true garlic-lover's recipe, one in which the allium plays a leading role. There's no need to be intimidated by the amount of garlic here—it loses all its bite as it boils alongside the potatoes, becoming mellow and sweet.

In this recipe—as at the Diner—we use a food mill to make our mashed potatoes as smooth and creamy as possible, but if you don't have access to a food mill, a potato masher works just fine. Just keep at it, mashing and smashing until you've eliminated all the lumps.

2½ pounds (about 8 medium) **waxy potatoes** (we use Yukon Golds), peeled and cut into large chunks

10 **garlic cloves**

1 tablespoon **kosher salt**, plus more to taste

½ cup (1 stick) **unsalted butter**, cold, cut into 4 pieces

½ cup **whole milk**, warmed

½ teaspoon **ground white pepper**

1. Place the potatoes and garlic in a large pot, and add the salt and enough water to cover by 2 inches. Set over high heat and bring to a rolling boil, then reduce the heat to medium. Cook until the potatoes begin to come apart when pierced with a fork, 25 to 30 minutes. Set a colander in the sink, and carefully drain the potatoes and garlic into it.

2. Return the drained potatoes and garlic to the pot and cover with a clean kitchen towel. Let sit for 5 to 7 minutes (this allows most of the residual moisture to come off the potatoes, which permits the potatoes to absorb fat).

3. Pour the potatoes and garlic into a food mill set over a large mixing bowl, adding the butter before you begin cranking. (If you're not using a food mill, cut the butter into small cubes and drop into the potatoes before mashing by hand.) Process all the potatoes, then stir in the warm milk and white pepper until combined. Add salt to taste and serve.

2 pounds red new potatoes, cut into bite-sized chunks

2 tablespoons olive oil

1 teaspoon finely chopped fresh rosemary

1 teaspoon finely chopped fresh thyme

Kosher salt and freshly ground **black pepper**

SUMMER'S BLISS NEW POTATOES

Serves 4 as a side

When new potatoes are, well, new (a.k.a. really freshly dug), they're sweet, dense, and almost creamy, with a flavor utterly unlike potatoes that have been stored for some time. When you catch freshly dug thin-skinned potatoes in a high summer market, use a light hand in their preparation. Simply boil them in salty water or roast them, as we do here, amplifying their natural sweetness.

Don't be afraid to handle your produce at market! Freshly dug new potatoes are extremely firm and have almost no give when you squeeze them. As they begin to lose their natural moisture—which they need to if they're to store well—they start to yield more to the touch.

1. Preheat the oven to 400°F and line a baking sheet with aluminum foil.

2. In a large mixing bowl, toss the potatoes with the olive oil to coat. Add the rosemary and thyme, then sprinkle the salt (at least ½ teaspoon) and freshly ground pepper over the top.

3. Spread the potatoes evenly across the baking sheet. Slide the sheet into the oven and roast until the potatoes are slightly browned but still firm, about 25 minutes.

ROASTED HIGH-SEASON CORN

Serves 4 as a side

1 tablespoon **olive oil**

4 ears **fresh corn**, shucked

Kosher salt

Aside from boiling in hot, salty water, this is the best way we know to prepare peak-season corn. Roasting brings out corn's natural sweetness, and oven-roasting slightly caramelizes some of the sugars near the kernel's surface, imparting a satisfying snap when you chomp down.

Use only the freshest corn for this recipe. Corn's sugars begin to retreat into the cob the moment the ears are picked, meaning the longer it's been off the stalk, the starchier and less flavorful it'll be. Learn to be picky, buying corn from farms that grow their own and asking for the newest arrival (which you'll often find at the bottom of the heap).

1. Preheat the oven to 400°F and line a baking sheet with aluminum foil.

2. Rub a bit of the olive oil onto each ear of corn, to prevent it from sticking. Sprinkle lightly with salt and rub across the surface.

3. Lay the ears on the baking sheet. Roast in the oven, undisturbed, for 15 minutes, until the corn is glossy, the kernels have plumped, and their yellow color has intensified. Serve hot.

Kosher salt

8 ounces **wax beans**, topped and tailed

8 ounces **green beans**, topped and tailed

¼ cup **crème fraîche**

3 tablespoons **sherry vinegar**

3 tablespoons **extra-virgin olive oil**

2 tablespoons chopped **fresh dill**

1 **fennel bulb**, fronds removed, sliced paper-thin crosswise

Freshly ground **black pepper**

WAX BEANS AND FENNEL
WITH DILL

Serves 4 as a side

As summer kicks into high gear, so does the Diner's busiest season. But for many of our guests, summertime is long on relaxation and filled with simple pleasures—long hikes, dips in the swimming holes that dot the Catskills, and afternoon visits to a farmstand or backyard garden to gather supplies for a simple supper. This salad fits the bill. Wax beans, fennel, and dill all come into season just as school lets out in these parts. Refreshing, bright, and full of flavor, this recipe makes use of summer's ample produce and doesn't require much time near a hot stove.

Fennel, while delicious, can be a bit tough when eaten raw. A mandoline is helpful for slicing the bulbs into thin, translucent slices.

1. Bring a large pot of heavily salted water to a rapid boil over high heat. Make an ice bath by filling a large bowl halfway with ice cubes and adding water just to the level of the ice.

2. Gently drop the wax and green beans into the boiling water and stir to submerge. Cook until the beans are tender but still crisp, 3 to 4 minutes (carefully pull one out and taste to test). Use a slotted spoon to transfer them to the ice bath. When the beans are fully chilled, transfer to a strainer to drain.

3. In a large bowl, whisk together the crème fraîche, sherry vinegar, olive oil, and dill. Add the beans and fennel, season with salt and pepper, and mix thoroughly. Chill for at least 30 minutes before serving.

CLASSIC COLESLAW

Serves 6 to 8 as a side

The name "coleslaw" comes from the Dutch *kool sla*, which means, quite simply, "cabbage salad." The Dutch once ran things around here, so it seems appropriate to celebrate one of their signature dishes which, curiously, is more often associated with parts Southern. But regardless of origin, one thing's for certain: there are many ways with slaw, and tastes are as personal and varied as pizza slices in New York and fried chicken, well, everywhere.

Calling a coleslaw "classic" is bound to stir controversy. But this slaw truly sits in neutral, familiar territory—fresh cabbage and shredded carrot, seasoned with celery seed and mixed with slaw's three most common dressing ingredients: mayonnaise, mustard, and vinegar. Though this version is both quite creamy and satisfyingly crunchy, we don't claim superiority or perfection in this department; play with the proportions as you see fit, using this recipe as a jumping-off point.

Salting the cabbage overnight not only helps season the slaw but it also pulls some of the water out of the cabbage so that your end product is crisp and doesn't continue to weep, turning your slaw into a runny mess.

1 large head of **green cabbage**

1 tablespoon **kosher salt**

1 medium **carrot**, coarsely grated

1 cup **mayonnaise**

1 tablespoon **Dijon mustard**

3 tablespoons **apple cider vinegar**

2 teaspoons **celery seeds**

2 teaspoons freshly ground **black pepper**

1. Remove the tough outer leaves of the cabbage, then cut it into quarters and remove the core. Thinly slice the cabbage and place it in a large bowl. Sprinkle the salt over the top and mix thoroughly. Cover with plastic wrap and set in the fridge at least 4 hours, and up to overnight.

2. Squeeze the cabbage to remove excess water and transfer to a clean bowl. Add the carrot. In a small bowl, combine the mayonnaise, mustard, vinegar, celery seeds, and pepper. Pour the dressing over the cabbage and carrots, and mix well. For the best flavor, cover the slaw with plastic wrap and chill for a couple of hours before serving.

6 large **russet potatoes**

Vegetable oil, for frying

Kosher salt

PHOENICIA DINER FRENCH FRIES

Serves 4 as a side

Making fries at home is an intimidating task, but so worth it. For really crisp fries, soaking the potatoes overnight is key. The goal is to remove excess starch to get a crunchy exterior and a soft, almost creamy interior.

To work ahead, prep the potatoes the day or morning before you plan to eat. All you'll have left to do, then, is heat your oil and fry a few batches for a few minutes apiece to achieve the perfect complement to a burger, fried fish, or any other sandwich you like.

1. Fill a large bowl with water. Peel the potatoes, and place them in the water to prevent browning. Working one at a time, cut the potatoes lengthwise, first into ¼-inch-thick slices, then again into ¼-inch-thick fries. Return the sliced potatoes to the bowl of water and leave them in the fridge to soak for at least 8 hours or, better yet, overnight. (For shatteringly crisp fries, if you're not sound asleep during the soak, change the soaking water once to help pull even more starch from the potatoes.)

2. When you're ready to cook, remove the fries from the water and place them on towels to dry.

3. In a deep pot or Dutch oven, add enough oil to achieve a depth of 6 inches and heat the oil to 350°F (using a candy thermometer) over medium-high heat. Line a baking sheet with paper towels.

4. Working in batches (you want the fries to be able to bump about freely in the pot rather than be tightly packed), cook the fries until they are soft but haven't taken on any color, 3 to 4 minutes. Using a large slotted spoon, remove the fries from the oil and transfer to the paper towel–lined baking sheet. Repeat with all remaining fries.

5. Crank the heat up to high to increase the oil's temperature to 400°F. Have a large bowl at the ready.

6. Working in batches, add the fries, being sure not to overfill your pot (you don't want oil splattering and splashing over the top). Cook, leaving the fries alone, until golden brown and crisp, 2 to 3 minutes. Transfer the fries to a bowl and season with salt. Eat immediately.

BEER-BATTERED ONION RINGS

Serves 4 as a side

Onion rings are one of those restaurant pleasures most of us never think to attempt at home. They seem intimidatingly difficult, but they're not. Light and almost shatteringly crisp, these onion rings are absolutely addictive and well worth the effort. The secrets here are in the ratio of flour to cornstarch, and in the slight kick from both cayenne and paprika. Serve up a plate of these, hot from the fryer, and watch them disappear.

2 large **onions**, sliced into ½-inch-thick rings

1½ cups **all-purpose flour**

¾ cup **cornstarch**

1 teaspoon **cayenne**

1 teaspoon **sweet Spanish paprika**

1 tablespoon **kosher salt**, plus more for seasoning

½ teaspoon freshly ground **black pepper**

2 cups (16 ounces) **light, crisp beer**, like a lager or pilsner

Vegetable oil, for frying (see Note)

Ketchup, Sriracha sauce, or **other dipping sauce**, for serving

1. Sort through the sliced onions and remove the papery inner rings and any broken pieces. Reserve for stock or other uses.

2. In a large mixing bowl, combine the flour, cornstarch, cayenne, paprika, salt, and pepper and whisk together to blend well. Slowly add 12 ounces (1½ cups) of the beer while whisking vigorously until you achieve a thick pourable but still lumpy batter. Place the batter in the refrigerator for 30 minutes to rest and chill.

3. Fill a heavy-bottomed pot or Dutch oven with vegetable oil to a depth of 6 inches. Heat the oil to 350°F over medium-high heat. Line a large bowl or baking sheet with paper towels, and set it beside the stove.

4. Whisk the batter again vigorously to eliminate any large clumps. Add more beer in small amounts, as needed, until you've achieved a thick smooth batter (it does not hold its shape, but a finger dipped in stays liberally coated—thicker than heavy cream but thinner than cake frosting).

5. Working one at a time, dip an onion ring into the batter and turn to fully coat. Using your fingers, lift the ring from the batter and allow the excess batter to drip off, then lower into the oil, being careful not to splatter yourself. Repeat with more rings, working in small batches and making sure not to crowd the rings or overfill the fryer (you don't want the rings to lie stacked on one another, or for the temperature to drop by more than 25 degrees). Cook the rings on one side until they are a deep tan color and crispy, 2 to 3 minutes.

6. Use a slotted spoon or metal spatula to carefully turn the rings over, then cook on the other side until they're crackly, crispy, and a deep golden brown, another 2 to 3 minutes.

7. Use a slotted spoon to transfer the rings to the paper-lined bowl or baking sheet, and season with more salt. Before beginning a new batch, bring your oil back up to 350°F. Repeat until all the rings are cooked. Serve immediately with ketchup or other dipping sauce.

NOTE: Before you get all set up to make these, only to find out you're short on oil, pour water into the pot you plan to fry these in to figure out how much oil you'll need to achieve the desired depth for frying. If you make these onion rings enough times to realize you can't live without them, a tabletop deep fryer may be a good investment.

PIES, PUDDINGS, AND SWEETS

Ingredients

2¼ cups **all-purpose flour**

1 teaspoon **baking soda**

1 teaspoon **kosher salt**

1 cup (2 sticks) **unsalted butter**, softened

¾ cup packed **dark brown sugar**

¾ cup **granulated sugar**

2 large **eggs**, at room temperature

1 teaspoon **vanilla extract**

8 ounces **dark chocolate** (68% cocoa or higher), broken into large chunks

CHOCOLATE CHUNK COOKIES

Makes 8 very large cookies

Fruition Chocolate, located just a few miles down Route 28 from the Diner, is a bean-to-bar chocolate company run by two locals: head chocolatier Bryan Graham and his wife, Dahlia Rissman Graham. Bryan grew up learning to cook at his grandmother's Upstate farm, and developed a penchant for chocolate, specifically while training at the Culinary Institute of America—just a bit south and across the river in Hyde Park—and during an externship at the renowned Jacques Torres Chocolates in New York City. Dahlia grew up nearby, and after leaving for college and spending a year teaching in Peru, returned home with Bryan to start both a business and a family. We feature their superb chocolate in many of our desserts, as well as our hot chocolate. If you can't make it up to our neck of the woods, you can mail-order Fruition's award-winning chocolate, or substitute another high-quality dark chocolate.

These cookies are a favorite of visitors preparing for a long drive home. Huge, soft in the middle, crisp on the bottom, and full of large chunks of dark chocolate throughout, the cookies are a perfect afternoon pick-me-up—or a small meal itself. They're delicious with a bracing cup of coffee or black tea, but their texture lends them to milk-dunking, as they'll soak up some of the liquid without becoming too soggy. So, may we suggest a tall glass of cold milk as the perfect, classic pairing?

1. In a small mixing bowl, mix the flour, baking soda, and salt. Set aside.

2. In the bowl of a stand mixer with a paddle attachment, place the butter, brown sugar, and granulated sugar. Beat on low speed until the butter and sugar have begun to form a smooth paste, 5 minutes. Scrape down the bowl and paddle. Increase the speed to medium-high and beat until the volume begins to increase and the mixture begins to lighten and become fluffier, another 5 minutes. Scrape down the bowl and paddle again. Increase the speed to high, and beat until fluffy and khaki-colored, another 5 minutes.

3. Decrease the speed to medium and add the eggs one at a time, making sure the first egg is fully incorporated before adding the second. Once the second egg is incorporated, add the vanilla. Turn off the mixer.

RECIPE CONTINUES ➻

4. Add the dry ingredients, then beat on low speed, just until the dough comes together. Add the chocolate pieces and mix just until they're evenly distributed, another 30 seconds. (At this point, the dough can either be wrapped in plastic and kept in the refrigerator for up to a week, or frozen and kept for 3 months.)

5. Line a baking sheet with parchment paper. Divide the dough into 8 portions, each one roughly 5 ounces. Roll each portion into a ball and place on the lined sheet, leaving a minimum of 4 inches between each cookie (depending on the size baking sheets you have, you may need a second baking sheet to accommodate this spacing). Chill the cookies on their sheet in the fridge until they are firm again, at least 30 minutes and up to overnight. (If chilling longer than 1 hour, cover loosely with plastic wrap to avoid drying out the dough.)

6. When you're ready to bake, position a rack in the center of the oven, and preheat the oven to 350°F.

7. Bake the cookies on the middle rack for 8 minutes and then rotate the baking sheet. Bake until the cookies are dark golden brown, another 10 to 12 minutes. Allow the cookies to cool on their sheet until firm enough to handle (5 to 10 minutes), then transfer to a wire cooling rack until you can't resist anymore.

OATMEAL PECAN COOKIES

Makes 8 very large cookies

2 cups **pecan pieces**

1¼ cups **all-purpose flour**

2 cups **old-fashioned rolled oats**

1 teaspoon **ground cinnamon**

¼ teaspoon **ground cardamom**

1 teaspoon **baking soda**

1 teaspoon **kosher salt**

1 cup (2 sticks) **unsalted butter**, softened

¾ cup packed **dark brown sugar**

¾ cup **granulated sugar**

2 large **eggs**, at room temperature

1 teaspoon **vanilla extract**

A hefty, cakey round—somewhere between a muffin and a chewy cookie in both sweetness and texture—these make for a meal in and of themselves. And who's to say you shouldn't? With plenty of oats and pecans to keep you going, they can even pass as breakfast. If you can't quite justify that, though, you may want to pace yourself and save room for one of these as a substantial dessert.

1. Position a baking rack in the center of the oven and preheat the oven to 300°F.

2. Spread the nuts in a single layer on an unlined baking sheet. Toast for 5 minutes, then stir lightly to redistribute the nuts. Toast until the nuts are lightly browned and fragrant, another 3 to 4 minutes.

3. In a medium bowl, stir together the flour, oats, cinnamon, cardamom, baking soda, and salt.

4. In the bowl of a stand mixer with a paddle attachment, beat the butter, brown sugar, and granulated sugar on low speed until a smooth paste begins to form, 5 minutes. Scrape down the bowl and paddle. Increase the speed to medium-high and beat until the volume begins to increase and the mixture begins to lighten and become fluffier, another 5 minutes. Scrape down the bowl and paddle again. Increase the speed to high, and beat until fluffy and khaki colored, another 5 minutes.

5. Decrease the speed to medium and add the eggs one at a time, making sure the first egg is fully incorporated before adding the second. Once the second egg is incorporated, add the vanilla. Turn off the mixer.

6. Add the dry ingredients, then beat on low speed just until the dough comes together. Add the pecan pieces and mix until they're evenly distributed, another 30 seconds. (At this point, the dough can either be wrapped in plastic and kept in the refrigerator for up to 1 week or frozen and kept for 3 months.)

7. Line a baking sheet with parchment paper. Divide the dough into 8 portions, each one roughly 5 ounces. Roll each portion into a ball and place on the lined sheet, leaving a minimum of 4 inches between each cookie. (Depending on the size of the baking sheets, you may need a second to accommodate this spacing.)

8. Chill the cookies on their baking sheet in the fridge until they are firm again, at least 30 minutes and up to overnight. (If chilling longer than an hour, cover loosely with plastic wrap to avoid drying out the dough.)

9. When you're ready to bake, position a baking rack in the center of the oven, and preheat the oven to 350°F.

10. Bake on the middle rack for 8 minutes and then rotate the cookie sheet. Bake until the cookies are dark golden brown, another 10 to 12 minutes. Allow the cookies to cool on their sheet until they've firmed up enough to handle (5 to 10 minutes), then transfer them to a wire cooling rack until you can't resist anymore.

THE PHOENICIA DINER GUIDE TO BAKERY-PERFECT MUFFINS

We always have a batch of freshly baked muffins on display at the counter; in diner speak, they're the universal sign of welcome. Split in half, buttered, and toasted on the griddle is the diner way. You can replicate that experience at home by toasting your halved muffins in a heavy-bottomed skillet over medium heat until they've developed a crunchy, golden crust. It only takes a couple of minutes.

Here are a few notes before re-creating these at home: All muffin tins are not made equal. There are many different sizes, which is why recipes can seem frustratingly inaccurate when it comes to predicting yield. Today, in the United States, a "standard" muffin cup ranges from 3½ to 4 ounces, but if you happen to have a muffin tin passed down from a baking relative, yours may well be smaller. Jumbo muffins have also come in and out of vogue in recent years, so there are larger tins floating about as well. At the Diner, the cups of our "standard" muffin tins each hold a scant 4 fluid ounces, which is what these recipes are based upon.

Muffin-baking is a great reason to invest in an oven thermometer, if you don't already have one (two is even better, as placing each in a different area of your oven will help you identify hot or cold spots, which can lead to uneven cooking). If you find your oven runs on the cooler side or heats unevenly, or if you favor an extra-crispy muffin top, you may want to crank your oven's temperature up an extra 25°F for the final stretch of baking—muffins should develop their golden-brown hue during the final minutes of baking.

When it comes to testing doneness in muffins, always use the trusty toothpick test, not your eyes. Various flours, differing moisture and density levels, and a whole host of other ingredients mean a "done" muffin can look, and even feel, all kinds of different ways. But when a toothpick inserted into the center of the muffin comes out clean, you know the baking's done.

AUTUMN HARVEST MUFFINS

Makes 12 muffins

These are barely sweet, a hearty and, yes, healthy muffin, the sort of thing you can feel good about starting your day with or having with a cup of coffee or tea as an afternoon pick-me-up.

1. Position a rack in the center of the oven, and preheat the oven to 375°F. Lightly grease a 12-cup muffin tin.

2. In a large bowl, sift together the flours, brown sugar, baking powder, baking soda, salt, and spices, making sure everything is well distributed.

3. In a small bowl, whisk together the milk, eggs, coconut oil, and vanilla until smooth. Stir in the carrot, apple, raisins, pecans, and coconut. Add the milk mixture to the flour mixture. Use a rubber spatula to fold the dry ingredients into the liquid just until the mixture comes together; don't overmix. The batter will be quite thick and chunky.

4. Using a large ice cream scoop or half-cup dry measuring cup, scoop the muffin batter into the muffin cups until they are filled to the rims but not overflowing. Sprinkle the oats evenly over the tops of the muffins.

5. Bake for 10 minutes, then rotate the pan 180 degrees. Bake until they are the color of hay, and a toothpick inserted into the center comes out clean, another 5 minutes or so.

6. Let the muffins rest in their tins just until they've cooled enough to handle and have pulled away from the pan a hair, about 10 minutes, then transfer them to a wire cooling rack. (Once cooled, the muffins will keep at room temperature for 2 to 3 days if wrapped tightly or stored in an airtight container.)

Unsalted butter, vegetable oil, or non-stick baking spray, for greasing the muffin tins

1 cup all-purpose flour

2 cups whole wheat flour

½ cup packed dark brown sugar

1 tablespoon baking powder

1 teaspoon baking soda

1 teaspoon kosher salt

1 teaspoon ground cinnamon

½ teaspoon ground ginger

½ teaspoon ground allspice

¼ teaspoon grated nutmeg

¼ teaspoon ground cloves

1½ cups whole milk

3 large eggs

½ cup coconut oil, melted

2 teaspoons vanilla extract

½ cup coarsely grated carrot

½ cup coarsely grated apple

½ cup raisins

½ cup chopped pecans, toasted

¼ cup unsweetened shredded coconut

½ cup old-fashioned rolled oats

BLUEBERRY-GINGER BUTTERMILK MUFFINS

Makes 18 muffins

In summer, the Hudson Valley is awash with berries—U-Pick fields, roadside stands, and farmers markets offer up more berries than we could ever eat fresh. So, of course, we put them into everything—piling them onto French toast, stirring them into pancakes and waffles, and baking them into pies, crisps, and these muffins. These are the most "refined" muffins we serve—light in the crumb, with clean, classic flavors. There are no tricks here, save for a little zing of fresh ginger to make things interesting.

1. Position a rack in the center of the oven, and preheat to 375°F. Lightly grease an 18-cup muffin tin.

2. In a large bowl, sift together the flour, sugar, baking powder, salt, and ground ginger. Add the blueberries and stir gently to combine.

3. In a medium bowl, whisk together the buttermilk, eggs, fresh ginger, lemon zest, vanilla, and melted butter. Add the buttermilk mixture to the dry ingredients. Use a rubber spatula to gently fold the dry ingredients into the wet, just until the mixture comes together.

4. Scoop the muffin batter into the muffin cups until they are filled to just below the rim. Bake for 10 minutes, then rotate the pan 180 degrees. Bake until the muffins are a golden straw color and a toothpick inserted into the center comes out clean, another 10 to 15 minutes.

5. Let the muffins rest in the tin just until they've cooled enough to handle and have pulled away from the pan a hair—about 10 minutes—then transfer to a wire rack. (Once cooled, these will keep at room temperature for 2 to 3 days if wrapped tightly or stored in an airtight container.)

Unsalted butter, vegetable oil, or nonstick baking spray, for greasing the muffin tins

4 cups all-purpose flour

¾ cup sugar

1 tablespoon baking powder

½ teaspoon kosher salt

1 tablespoon ground ginger

1 cup fresh blueberries

2 cups buttermilk

4 large eggs

1 tablespoon finely grated fresh ginger

1 teaspoon grated lemon zest

1 teaspoon vanilla extract

½ cup (1 stick) unsalted butter, melted

WHOLE WHEAT-COCONUT BANANA BREAD

Makes one 8½ by 4½-inch loaf

1 cup **whole wheat flour**

⅔ cup **all-purpose flour**, plus 1 tablespoon for dusting

1 teaspoon **baking powder**

½ teaspoon **kosher salt**

½ teaspoon **ground cinnamon**

½ teaspoon **ground ginger**

1 cup **sugar**

2 large **eggs**, at room temperature

½ cup plus 1 tablespoon **coconut oil**, melted

1½ cups very ripe **banana**, mashed (about 3 large bananas)

¼ cup **crème fraîche**

1 teaspoon grated **lemon zest**

1 teaspoon **vanilla extract**

¾ cup **pecan pieces**, lightly toasted

½ cup **unsweetened shredded coconut**

Banana bread: cakelike enough to indulge a sweet tooth but wholesome enough to still feel virtuous. It's a reminder that diner cooking is really just familiar, comforting home-style cooking done by someone else.

There are innumerable approaches with banana bread, but this is ours. Slightly chewy, luscious, and moist thanks to crème fraîche and coconut oil, and packed with satisfying nuts, shredded coconut, and plenty of banana, this banana bread works as well for breakfast as it does for a snack or dessert.

1. Position a rack in the center of the oven and preheat the oven to 350°F.

2. In a large bowl, sift together the whole wheat flour, ⅔ cup all-purpose flour, baking powder, salt, cinnamon, and ginger and whisk to blend everything together.

3. In the bowl of a stand mixer with the whisk attachment, place the sugar and eggs. Beat on high speed until pale and fluffy, about 5 minutes (alternatively, use a handheld electric mixer or even egg beaters for this, but plan to do it longer). Reduce to low speed and slowly drizzle in ½ cup coconut oil (it doesn't matter if there are small globules of coconut oil distributed in the batter or it doesn't look uniformly integrated; coconut oil is unruly that way). While still mixing on low speed, add the bananas, crème fraîche, lemon zest, and vanilla. Turn the speed back up to high and mix just until everything comes together, a minute or so.

4. Remove the bowl from the stand and gently fold in the flour mixture. Add the pecan pieces and coconut and continue to fold the mixture until there are no streaks of flour and the pecans and coconut are evenly distributed.

5. Pour 1 tablespoon coconut oil into an 8½ by 4½-inch (1 pound) loaf pan and use a paper towel to grease the bottom and sides. Add 1 tablespoon all-purpose flour and shake the pan to evenly dust the bottom and sides.

6. Pour the batter into the loaf pan. Bake until the banana bread is slightly crispy, golden brown on the top, with a crack down the middle and a toothpick inserted into the middle comes out clean, about 1 hour. Remove it from the oven and carefully turn the loaf out of the pan onto a baking rack to cool right away. Allow to cool at least 1 hour before slicing. (The unsliced bread keeps, tightly wrapped in plastic, for 3 days, or freeze, wrapped tightly, in its entirety. Unwrap frozen bread—otherwise, it sweats—and leave at room temp to thaw.)

Simpson Memorial Ski Slope and Skiing in the Catskills

It was winter 1932, and the Lake Placid Winter Olympics were the talk of the town in New York State. Three friends—Lloyd Kinsey, Carroll Simpson, and Paul Miller—watched as men glided across the snow and flew through the air over large snow mounds with long, thin blades of wood attached to their feet. The athletes were skiing, and the boys were captivated.

Back home in Phoenicia, the Depression carried on. In summertime, the boarders came, spending their money and boosting the economy as they breathed fresh mountain air, hunted, and fished. But winters were tough in the Catskills hamlet: overland travel was difficult in all that snow, and most of the region's economic activities—stripping bark for tanning, farming, and fishing—ground to a halt in the cold months. For many in the region, winter was a season to be survived by careful planning and belt tightening. But these three boys had an idea: to bring skiing to little Phoenicia.

The old logging roads were a good start for sliding through the snowy woods and down gently sloping hillsides, but the particular thrills seemed to lie in whizzing downhill, even over a jump, perhaps.

Carroll Simpson was one of three brothers whose family owned a large tract of land spread across several hills on either side of Esopus Creek. The slopes were rife with hickories, whose bark was used in the family business, the Phoenix Tannery. Carroll and his brothers, Jim and Mickey, nagged their mother, Clara, until she agreed to donate a few acres to the state. The boys in FDR's newly formed Civilian Conservation Corps (CCC), which had set up a camp in nearby Margaretville, would clear a slope. They would name the place after their late father, Jay Simpson.

In February 1935, the first enthusiastic amateurs huffed uphill for a quick whoosh down Simpson Memorial Ski Slope, the first downhill ski area in the state. The Simpson boys knew right away they were on to something.

The word was out, and the boys and some friends and neighbors spent that summer scheming improvements. They rented an industrial engine and rigged a motored rope tow to pull people up the hill, a sort of crazy-quilt contraption with a bend in the line that demanded skiers let go, walk a short ways, and then grab hold again for the second leg. A group formed the Phoenicia Ski Club and built a small lodge where skiers could warm up and purchase refreshments. But they needed more patrons.

Down in New York City, excitement about

skiing—a European sport then new to Americans—was taking hold among the well-to-do. Saks Fifth Avenue was selling and renting skis, hiring Scandinavian instructors to pass along some basic skills, and had even built an indoor ski slide and covered it with "snow" made from borax soap.

Enthusiasm was growing around the new winter sport, but Phoenicia needed to find a way to attract folks to visit. The town already had railroad tracks; they'd been built to transport raw hides up to the Catskills and tanned hides and other goods back down to Kingston's river port or straight to the warehouses of New York City. In 1936, the first ski train ran from Weehawken, New Jersey, right into little Phoenicia. Drivers in their cars awaited the passengers and shuttled the skiers to the slope. The slope's success was a phenomenon: one day, the trains overwhelmed the little town, bringing 1,496 winter tourists. Suddenly, boardinghouses were full and any town resident with a spare room had a renter. Visitors wanted to extend their ski weekend rather than make the long round trip in a day. (It's always been hard to leave these mountains.)

The brothers all held full-time jobs, but these were mountain boys, resourceful and hardworking. They spent weeks mowing the slope in summer, and used snowshoes strapped to their feet to pack the ski runs in winter. World War II brought gasoline rations, which presented a challenge in keeping the tow motor running. Carroll, Mickey, and Jim scrimped and saved their stamps, pooling enough gasoline to open the slope at least one weekend per winter. Meanwhile, nearby Belleayre Mountain hosted its inaugural ski season in 1949, with a dozen trails, a rope tow, a lodge at the summit, a cafeteria, parking for 300 cars, and New York State's first chairlift.

By the skin of their teeth, the Simpson boys held on, keeping the slope in continuous operation year after year. But the 1960s brought change. In 1960, Hunter Mountain opened just a little way deeper into the hills. The advent of automated snowmaking arrived. Safety regulations were enforced and insurance rates soared. With a little cash on hand, the brothers expanded the slope's terrain and improved the lodge, adding a kitchen with a grill. They knew they would need more to compete with the flashier ski areas that were opening in the region.

The Simpson brothers tried to keep up, attempting to sell stock to raise money to expand their slope's terrain and amenities, but there were few takers. The Small Business Administration proved of little help—investing in a small, family-run ski slope was too risky. Carroll passed away in 1965, and Jim followed in 1971. Left to his own devices, Mickey decided 1979 would be the slope's last hurrah. He was seventy-five years old.

While the Simpsons' heyday has faded from view, the family is responsible for making this region a stronghold in winter sports, one that continues to grow as the region resurges. New investment has brought updates to Hunter Mountain's ski facilities. Belleayre has a new high-speed gondola and is, at the time of this writing, in the midst of being developed into a year-round recreational resort, with a pesticide-free golf course, LEED-certified hotel buildings, and Highmount Spa, named for the town that was once home to some of the state's most extravagant summer residences, and a hub of arts and culture. Though controversial, the development's allure is its boost for regional employment (particularly in the shoulder seasons) and the badly needed lodging amenities for the ever-growing number of year-round tourists.

At the time of this writing, Mickey's son, Jay, is nearly as old as his father was when he sold the slope. Jay moved downriver decades ago, seeking work. But he comes back to Phoenicia often, where he's held on to a bit of hillside—his little patch of heaven and his past—and always detours off Route 28 to gaze up at the now-dormant slope and to remember.

CHOCOLATE-PEANUT BUTTER PIE
WITH RITZ CRACKER CRUST

Makes one 9-inch pie

This salty-sweet, decadent pie is a hybrid of old-school diner classics—chocolate chess pie and peanut butter pie—and it has developed a devoted following. The mousse, which spotlights the high-quality local chocolate from our neighbors at Fruition Chocolate, is rich but not too dense, and the smooth filling is offset by the slightly salty, crumbly-crunchy Ritz cracker crust that Sara suggested when Chef Chris was first playing around with this recipe.

Any smooth peanut butter will do, but we like Peter Pan. Chris grew up on it and has had a soft spot for it ever since. Natural peanut butters will lower the sugar content here, but the texture won't come out as smooth and light. We use bar chocolate for this recipe, but if you're using chocolate chips, you'll need approximately 1⅓ cups.

The two-step process of incorporating the cream into the chocolate is essential to achieve the light, fluffy texture of the mousse: the first, vigorous addition lightens the chocolate mixture, and the second, gentle folding utilizes the billowy texture of the whipped cream to give the mousse its essential lift.

FOR THE CRUST

2 sleeves **original Ritz crackers** (about 30 crackers)

1 tablespoon plus 1½ teaspoons **dark brown sugar**, packed

4 tablespoons **unsalted butter**, melted

FOR THE MOUSSE

8 ounces 65–70% high-quality **dark chocolate**, broken into small pieces (or 1⅓ cups chocolate chips)

1 cup **creamy peanut butter**

2 cups **heavy cream**

2 tablespoons **granulated sugar**

1 teaspoon **vanilla extract**

¼ cup **roasted salted peanuts**, chopped

1. **Make the crust:** Place the crackers and brown sugar in a food processor and blitz until the crackers reach a fine, sandy consistency; you'll have about 1 packed cup. Slowly drizzle in the melted butter and process for another 15 seconds to evenly incorporate.

2. Spread the buttered crumbs evenly in an 9-inch pie plate and use your fingertips to press them firmly against the bottom and sides. Place the crust in the freezer, uncovered, for at least

1 hour to chill and set. (This can be done well in advance, but if leaving the crust untended for more than an hour or two, wrap in plastic or gently press tin foil over the top of the crust to keep it from taking on other flavors from the freezer.)

3. **Make the mousse:** Put 2 inches of water into a saucepan or the bottom of a double boiler. Set over low heat and bring to a simmer. Place the chocolate in the top of the double boiler or in a medium metal bowl (make sure it

RECIPE CONTINUES ➥

227

completely covers the mouth of the saucepan, and that the bottom of the bowl doesn't touch the water), and melt the chocolate, stirring occasionally with a rubber spatula, until smooth. Add the peanut butter and mix thoroughly. Turn off the heat.

4. In the bowl of a stand mixer fitted with the whisk attachment, combine the cream, granulated sugar, and vanilla and whip on medium-high until stiff peaks form when you pull up the whisk. (Go slowly after the cream begins to hold its shape, being careful not to overmix.) You're looking to be able to spike the cream like Sonic the Hedgehog's hair. (Alternatively, use hand beaters or, if you're feeling energetic, a whisk.)

5. Remove the bowl of chocolate and peanut butter mixture from the pot and add one-third of the whipped cream. Using a rubber spatula, stir vigorously to lighten the mix. Add the remaining whipped cream and gently fold it in until there are no white streaks running through and all the cream is evenly incorporated.

6. **Assemble the pie:** Pour the mixture into the chilled crust and smooth around to the edges with the rubber spatula. Sprinkle the chopped peanuts over the pie. Place in the fridge to set for at least 1 hour before serving. (This pie keeps, tightly wrapped in the fridge, for up to 2 days.)

BOOZY BUTTERSCOTCH PUDDING

Serves 6

Puddings, generally, seem to have gone out of fashion—a disappointment for those of us devoted to these sweet, creamy meal-enders. If you're to find pudding anywhere these days, it's bound to be in a diner, where vanilla and chocolate are classic. But butterscotch is a cult favorite, and it belongs in the dessert case alongside the other greats. This one is silky smooth and a gorgeous golden color, fit for a celebration or just to sate the workaday sweet tooth.

3 tablespoons **cornstarch**

¾ cup packed **dark brown sugar**

Pinch of **kosher salt**

1½ cups **whole milk**

1½ cups **heavy cream**

3 large **egg yolks**

2 teaspoons **vanilla extract**

2 ounces **whiskey** or **Scotch** (see Note)

1 tablespoon **unsalted butter**

Unsweetened whipped cream, for serving (optional)

1. In a heavy-bottomed saucepan, whisk together the cornstarch, brown sugar, and salt. Add the milk and cream, then warm the mixture over medium heat, stirring constantly with a wooden spoon or rubber spatula. The mixture will begin to deepen in color after about 3 minutes, then turn fragrant soon thereafter. Continue cooking until the pudding begins to bubble and thicken, 10 to 12 minutes. Test your consistency by coating a spoon with the pudding and drawing a line with your finger through the pudding; if the line remains, the pudding is set, but if it runs back onto itself, continue to cook. When the spoon test succeeds, remove the pot from the heat.

2. In a small bowl, whisk together the egg yolks, vanilla, and whiskey. Slowly stream the egg yolk mixture into the warm pudding mixture, whisking constantly and vigorously, until everything has been incorporated. Return the pudding to the stove, and cook over low heat, stirring constantly, until the pudding is again thick enough to coat the spoon, about another 5 minutes.

3. Remove the pot from the heat and whisk in the butter. Divide the pudding among 6 small serving dishes, cover tightly with plastic, and chill in the refrigerator for at least 1 hour or up to overnight before serving. (The warm pudding will still be quite runny when fully cooked; it won't set up until after it has been thoroughly chilled. Keeps up to 5 days in the fridge.) If you like, serve with unsweetened whipped cream.

NOTE: The boozy flavor in this pudding is strong, intended to cut the unctuous sweetness of all the dairy. While butterscotch was originally made with, yes, Scotch, we recommend using a clean-tasting whiskey that hasn't been peated or otherwise infused with smoky flavors; save the complex stuff for drinking.

You should not serve this to alcohol avoiders or to children; the booze gets added toward the end of this recipe, and the gentle warming that happens after its addition isn't enough to cook out all the alcohol.

DARK CHOCOLATE PUDDING

Serves 6

The word *pudding* alone conjures nostalgia. In old-school bakeries and diners, you'll still find it in refrigerated dessert cases, the kind that sits on top of countertops, spinning lazily, or the long, clear cases that run at kids'-eye level, just right for pressing faces to the glass in hungry awe. Creamy, sweet, and just the right amount of gloopy, pudding is often marketed as food for children, with boxes of instant mix sitting alongside brightly colored Jell-O on supermarket shelves. But this is no elementary-school pudding. It's intense and silky, full of flavorful dark chocolate—just the sort of thing you wouldn't want to feed a kid before bedtime.

1 tablespoon **cornstarch**

2 tablespoons **cocoa powder**

¼ cup **sugar**

Pinch of **kosher salt**

1½ cups **whole milk**

1½ cups **heavy cream**

8 ounces 65–70% high-quality **dark chocolate**, finely chopped (or 1⅓ cups chocolate chips; see Note))

1 teaspoon **vanilla extract**

1 tablespoon **unsalted butter**

Unsweetened whipped cream, for serving (optional)

1. In a heavy-bottomed saucepan, whisk together the cornstarch, cocoa powder, sugar, and salt.

2. Add the milk and cream, then warm the mixture over medium heat, stirring frequently just until it begins to bubble. Allow to bubble for about 1 minute, then reduce the heat to low and cook, stirring frequently with a rubber spatula, until it thickens enough to coat the back of a spoon, 8 to 12 minutes.

3. Remove the pot from the heat and add the chopped chocolate. Whisk until the chocolate is fully melted and the pudding is smooth. Add the vanilla and butter and stir to incorporate. Divide the pudding among 6 small serving dishes and cover tightly with plastic wrap. Chill in the refrigerator for at least 1 hour or overnight before serving. (The warm pudding will still be quite runny when fully cooked; it won't set up until after it has been thoroughly chilled. The pudding will keep, covered, in the fridge for up to 5 days.) If you like, serve topped with unsweetened whipped cream.

NOTE: We use bars of the very fine chocolate from our neighbors at Fruition (see page 208), but if you can't find Fruition, use the best-quality dark chocolate, in the 65–70% cacao range, that you have access to (if you're using chocolate chips, you'll need about 1⅓ cups). Remember, superlative chocolate makes for superlative chocolate pudding.

DOWN-HOME BANANA PUDDING

Serves 8 to 10

Banana pudding is foreign to a lot of folks outside the American South, but Chef Chris has been on something of a campaign to introduce it to parts northern since he moved to New York more than two decades ago. Ubiquitous and beloved where he comes from, banana pudding is the sort of thing you see the component ingredients of stacked on display when you walk into grocery stores across the South. Its reputation is well earned: silky vanilla pudding, vanilla wafer cookies, sliced ripe bananas, and if you like, a big dollop of whipped cream. What's not to love?

1 (11-ounce) box **vanilla wafer cookies**

6 to 7 ripe **bananas**, (about 3 pounds), sliced into ½-inch rounds (see Note)

1½ cups **sugar**

½ cup **cornstarch**

½ teaspoon **kosher salt**

2 quarts **half-and-half**

2 tablespoons **vanilla extract**

Unsweetened whipped cream, for serving (optional)

1. Arrange half the vanilla wafers (about 40 cookies) in the bottom of a 2-inch-deep 10-inch-square baking dish or similarly deep dish with at least a 12-cup capacity (a standard 9 by 13-inch works fine here as well). Layer the bananas evenly on top of the wafers. Set the pan in the refrigerator to chill while you prepare the pudding.

2. In a large heavy-bottomed saucepan, whisk together the sugar, cornstarch, and salt. Pour in the half-and-half, then warm the mixture over medium heat, stirring frequently with a wooden spoon or rubber spatula until it begins to bubble and thicken, 10 to 12 minutes. To check if the pudding is ready, dip a spoon into the pudding and draw a line through the pudding with your finger. If the line remains, the pudding is set; if the pudding runs back onto itself, it needs to continue to cook a bit longer.

The warm pudding will still be quite runny when fully cooked; it won't set up until after it has been thoroughly chilled.

3. Stir in the vanilla, then remove the cookie and banana pan from the fridge and pour the warm pudding evenly over the wafers and fruit. Line the outer edge of the pan with a single layer of wafers pushed halfway down into the pudding. Coarsely chop the remaining wafers and sprinkle them over the surface of the pudding. Gently lay a piece of plastic wrap across the top and chill in the refrigerator for at least 2 hours, or up to 3 days. If you like, serve the pudding with a bowl of unsweetened whipped cream alongside.

NOTES: The assembly instructions here are for an old-school, family-style pudding. You can also serve it in individual dessert coupes or ramekins, but you may need to adjust the number of cookies and bananas slightly to account for the change.

For this recipe, you'll want to use perfectly ripe bananas—that is to say, bananas whose skins are bright yellow, not tinged with green or covered in brown spots; you want fruit that is fragrant and firm.

You can prepare the pudding up to 3 days in advance. Southerners prefer the cookies once they've softened and absorbed some of the flavors. If you prefer crispier cookies, wait until you're ready to serve to add them to the dessert.

LEMON MERINGUE PIE

Makes one 9-inch pie

Tart and elegant, lemon meringue is the queen of diner desserts. Set in a chrome and glass pie case, reaching high from her pedestal, this pie appears formidable, and almost too pretty to eat. She's a demanding confection, requiring attention and precision, and many consider a superlative lemon meringue pie the mark of a great diner.

The invention of lemon meringue pie is attributed to a Mrs. Elizabeth Goodfellow (1767–1851), the proprietress of America's first cooking school, in Philadelphia. Her lemon pudding called for ten egg yolks; the whites were put to use in a meringue topping. While the recipe has evolved far beyond Victorian-era tastes and techniques, this iteration pays homage to Mrs. Goodfellow's original recipe, calling for the same abundant number of egg yolks (most lemon meringue recipes use only four or five). This is a true lemon lover's filling: a thick, luscious lemon curd made almost neon yellow from the concentration of lemon zest and all those yolks.

. . . .

FOR THE CRUST

4 ounces **graham crackers**

6 tablespoons (¾ stick) **unsalted butter**, melted

2 tablespoons **all-purpose flour**

2 tablespoons **sugar**

1 teaspoon grated **lemon zest**

¼ teaspoon **kosher salt**

FOR THE LEMON CURD

10 large **egg yolks** (see Note)

5 tablespoons **cornstarch**

Juice and zest of 4 **lemons** (about ¾ cup juice)

1¼ cups **sugar**

¼ teaspoon **kosher salt**

¾ cup (1½ sticks) **unsalted butter**

NOTE: You'll be left with 5 egg whites after separating the eggs for the curd and meringue. Use the extra whites for a batch of meringue cookies or a pavlova, or simply keep them, covered, in the fridge for an egg-white omelet or scramble. And be sure to work quickly to make the meringue while the curd is still warm, as it'll adhere to the pie better.

1. Make the crust: Place the graham crackers in the bowl of a food processor and pulse until they are fine crumbs. Add the butter, flour, sugar, lemon zest, and salt to the bowl and process until the mixture is smooth, 15 seconds. (You should have about 1½ cups of crumbs.)

2. Pour the crumbs into a 9-inch pie dish. Use your hands to press the crumbs tightly and evenly along the bottom and up the sides of the dish. Put in the fridge to chill for at least 30 minutes.

3. Position a rack in the center of the oven and preheat the oven to 350°F.

4. Bake the crust until it begins to set, 7 to 9 minutes. Remove from the oven and set aside to cool.

5. Make the curd: In a large bowl, whisk together the egg yolks and cornstarch until they form a smooth paste.

6. In a heavy-bottomed nonreactive saucepan, stir together the lemon juice and zest, sugar, salt, and butter. Bring to a boil over high heat and stir until the sugar dissolves. Remove from the heat.

7. Slowly pour 1 cup of the lemon liquid into the egg yolk mixture while whisking rapidly to avoid curdling the yolks until combined. Add this mixture back to the pot, whisking vigorously, just to combine, as you go.

RECIPE CONTINUES ➽

5 large **egg whites**, at room temperature

¼ cup plus 1 tablespoon **sugar**

½ teaspoon **cornstarch**

¼ teaspoon **cream of tartar**

¼ teaspoon **vanilla extract**

Pinch of **kosher salt**

8. Return the pot to the stovetop and cook over medium heat, stirring constantly with a rubber spatula to avoid scorching the bottom or sides of the pot. If the mixture begins to clump, remove from the heat and whisk until it is smooth again. Cook until the curd is thick enough to coat the back of a spoon, 4 to 5 minutes. Pour into the cooled crust while the curd is still warm.

9. Make the meringue: Working quickly while the curd is still warm, place the egg whites in the bowl of a stand mixer with the whisk attachment. Whip on low speed until the whites are frothy. Increase the speed to medium and whip until the egg whites begin to form soft peaks. (The whites will make mounds that will hold their shape when you lift the whisk.)

10. In a small bowl combine the sugar, cornstarch, and cream of tartar. Sprinkle the sugar mixture into the egg whites 1 tablespoon at a time while the mixer is running. When all the sugar is added, increase the speed to medium-high. Add the vanilla and salt and whip until the egg whites are glossy and form stiff peaks. To test for doneness, pull the whisk out of the whites. Peaks should form that hold their shape with the tip folding back onto itself.

11. Gently pile the meringue onto the curd, making sure to spread it all the way to the crust so that the meringue won't shrink when you bake it. Use a spoon or small spatula to make decorative waves in the meringue. Place the pie back in the 350°F oven and bake until the meringue is golden brown and crisp on the outside, 12 to 15 minutes, turning halfway through. Remove from the oven and let cool for 1 hour before slicing.

STRAWBERRY RHUBARB CRISP

Serves 6 to 8

Make this crisp in that magical time in early summer when strawberries and rhubarb are both in season simultaneously. The mellow sweetness of the topping acts as a foil to the refreshingly tart citrus-accented berry and rhubarb base. Not overly sweet, this crisp works equally well served with a good dollop of plain yogurt as breakfast, or with vanilla ice cream or lightly sweetened whipped cream as dessert.

The crisp comes together in just a few minutes, but you do need to do a little prep the night before or morning of—slice up your rhubarb, toss with sugar, and let sit. This pulls out some of the moisture, which subdues rhubarb's sourness and keeps it more intact as it cooks.

1. **Start the filling:** In a large bowl, toss together the rhubarb and sugar. Cover and set in the fridge for 8 hours, or overnight.

2. **Make the topping:** In a large bowl, combine the oats, almond meal, brown sugar, salt, butter, yogurt, cinnamon, and ginger. Use a wooden spoon to vigorously mix the topping until thoroughly blended; it will be thick and sticky. Mash it flat against the sides of the bowl and put it in the freezer for 30 minutes to chill.

3. Position a rack in the center of the oven and preheat the oven to 325°F.

4. **Finish the filling:** Drain the rhubarb in a colander, discarding the liquid that's come off the fruit.

In another large bowl, combine the drained rhubarb, the strawberries, vanilla, maple syrup, cornstarch, and lemon zest and juice. Toss to combine.

5. Grease a 9 by 13-inch baking dish with the butter. Spread the fruit mixture evenly in the dish.

6. **Assemble the crisp:** Pull the crisp topping from the fridge. Using your hands, peel large pieces of the topping away from the sides of the mixing bowl and press them gently onto the surface of the fruit. Repeat until you've used up all the topping, working it gently with your hands until it almost entirely covers the fruit. No need to worry if you have a few gaps.

RECIPE CONTINUES ➤

FOR THE FILLING

4 cups **rhubarb**, cut into ½-inch pieces (about 6 large stalks)

¼ cup **sugar**

8 cups **fresh strawberries**, hulled and halved (if your berries are very large, quarter them)

1 teaspoon **vanilla extract**

½ cup **maple syrup**

⅓ cup **cornstarch**

Grated zest and juice of 1 **lemon**

1 tablespoon **unsalted butter**

FOR THE TOPPING

2 cups **old-fashioned rolled oats**

1½ cups **whole raw almonds**, pulsed to a coarse meal in a food processor (see Note, page 239)

⅔ cup packed **dark brown sugar**

½ teaspoon **kosher salt**

½ cup (1 stick) **unsalted butter**, melted

½ cup plain **whole-milk yogurt**

1 teaspoon **ground cinnamon**

1 teaspoon **ground ginger**

7. Set the baking dish on a rimmed baking sheet to catch any juice that bubbles over. Bake the crisp for 15 minutes, then rotate it 180 degrees and bake for another 15 minutes. Rotate a second time and bake until the fruit is bubbling and the topping is slightly browned and just barely crisped on top, another 10 to 15 minutes (40 to 45 minutes total).

8. Remove the crisp from the oven and let cool for at least 1 hour before serving. This gives the topping time to firm up significantly. If you like, serve the crisp topped with ice cream, freshly whipped cream, or yogurt.

FOR SERVING (OPTIONAL)

Lightly sweetened **whipped cream**

Vanilla ice cream

Plain yogurt

NOTE: If you don't feel like grinding your own almonds, you can substitute 2 cups store-bought almond meal.

For a nut-free option, substitute 2 cups rolled oats for the almonds, and pulse the oats several times in a food processor to create a coarse meal.

CRANBERRY CRUMBLE PIE

Makes one 9-inch pie

FOR THE CRUST

½ cup **ice cubes**

1 tablespoon **apple cider vinegar**

1¼ cups **all-purpose flour**, plus more for dusting

½ teaspoon **kosher salt**

2 teaspoons **sugar**

½ cup (1 stick) cold **unsalted butter**

FOR THE CRUMBLE TOPPING

1 cup **old-fashioned rolled oats**

½ cup packed **dark brown sugar**

¼ cup **all-purpose flour**

½ teaspoon **kosher salt**

½ teaspoon **ground ginger**

½ teaspoon **ground allspice**

1 teaspoon **ground cinnamon**

4 tablespoons (½ stick) **unsalted butter**, softened

For years, Chef Chris lived just a few blocks from the original Four & Twenty Blackbirds shop in Gowanus, Brooklyn, and he became not only a client of theirs but also a close friend of Emily and Melissa Elsen, the South Dakota–born sisters who run the place. They introduced him to his wife, Sara, who used to work for them. (Chris and Sara got married right there in the bright little corner shop.)

This pie is inspired by one of Four & Twenty's—a cranberry-sage pie they serve around Thanksgiving every year. It's got a bit of a cult following with its tart, earthy flavors, and it's a perfect dessert for those who don't like their treats too sweet. This pie riffs on the Elsens', balancing the sourness of the cranberries with a crumble topping and a little extra sugar in the pie dough.

While the folks at Four & Twenty are fanatical about making their pie crust by hand, at the Diner we do make the concession of using a food processor; not everyone can be as fantastically skilled and practiced as Emily and Melissa! If you don't have a food processor, use a pastry cutter or two knives. Just remember to work fast, as keeping your butter cold is the key to a flaky crust; and be careful not to overwork the dough, or it'll end up tough rather than tender.

. . . .

1. Make the crust: In a measuring cup or glass, combine ½ cup water, the ice cubes, and vinegar.

2. In the bowl of a food processor, combine the flour, salt, and sugar. Pulse a few times just to blend. Next, add the butter in small chunks (½-inch cubes or smaller). Pulse again, until the butter-flour mixture has turned crumbly (it's okay to have some larger pieces close to the size of peas). Running the food processor, slowly drizzle in enough of the water-vinegar mixture (no ice cubes) just to bind—about ¼ cup to start, adding little dribbles more, if needed. Turn off

the motor as soon as the dough begins to pull away from the sides. You will still have some loose floury bits; don't worry.

3. Lay a large piece of plastic wrap on a flat clean surface. Empty the contents of the food processor bowl into the center of the wrap, and quickly use the palms of your hands to shape the dough into a rough ball. Wrap the plastic tightly around the dough. Using the heel of one hand, press firmly down into the dough a couple of times to help smoosh the loose bits into the greater mass of dough. Gently pat the dough into

RECIPE CONTINUES ➻

1 pound (4 cups) **cranberries**, fresh or frozen (if using frozen, defrost before using, draining off any liquid that comes out of the cranberries)

1 small **tart apple** (Granny Smiths work well here), peeled and coarsely grated (roughly 1 cup)

¾ cup **maple syrup**

4 tablespoons **cornstarch**

½ teaspoon **kosher salt**

1 tablespoon **fresh lemon juice**

NOTES: To get all set up ahead of time, prepare the pie dough and the crumble topping the morning (or day before) you plan to bake your pie. All you'll have left to do is roll out the dough, mix the fruit filling, and sprinkle the crumble over the top.

Speaking of crumbles, here's a tip: chilling the topping helps keep the butter from immediately dribbling down into the fruit; instead, the chilling encourages it to stay up top with its fellow crumble ingredients long enough to bake into that caramel-like crunch we all long for.

The pie crust recipe makes a single crust, so if you're using it for a double crust or lattice pie, make sure to double the recipe.

a flattened disk, and chill in the fridge for a minimum of 2 hours, or overnight. (Alternatively, prepare the dough and freeze for up to 1 month. To thaw, transfer it to the fridge the night before you plan to use it.)

4. **Make the crumble topping:** In a medium bowl, combine the oats, brown sugar, flour, salt, ginger, allspice, and cinnamon. Using a fork, stir together to combine. Then, using your fingers, drop the butter, blob by blob, into the crumble mixture. Using your hands, mix the topping, squeezing a bit as you go, to create pebble-sized crumbles (there will be little bits of loose flour and spice mixture; don't worry). Cover the bowl and chill in the fridge at least 2 hours, or up to overnight.

5. When you're ready to go, take your pie dough from the fridge and let it warm up a bit, 5 to 10 minutes, until it's still very firm but yields under the press of a finger. On a well-floured work surface, roll the pie dough to a ¼-inch thickness and gently transfer and drape into a standard (not deep) 9-inch pie dish (your dough will be larger than the pie dish). Use your fingers to gently press the dough into the shape of the plate. Using a very sharp knife or kitchen shears, trim the extra dough away from the edge, leaving ½ inch of overhang all the way around. Chill in the refrigerator for 30 minutes.

6. **While the dough is chilling, prepare the filling:** In a medium bowl, combine the cranberries, apple, maple syrup, cornstarch, salt, and lemon juice and toss them together with a rubber spatula.

7. Position a rack in the center of the oven, and preheat the oven to 425°F. Line a rimmed baking sheet with aluminum foil.

8. Remove the pie crust from the fridge and use the flat edges of a fork's tines to press at a 45-degree angle in one direction all the way around the crust's edges, then coming back around at another 45-degree angle to make a cross-hatch pattern. Once you've "forked" your crust, use the palms of your hands to bring the remaining overhanging crust toward the edge of the pie plate, pressing gently to create a slight rim.

9. Pour the cranberry filling into the prepared crust, then top with the crumble, distributing it evenly across the cranberries and pressing down gently. Do your best to tuck all the cranberries under the crumble, as any left exposed to the heat of the oven will blacken.

10. Bake until the crust is just beginning to brown, 20 to 25 minutes. Rotate the pie 180 degrees, reduce the heat to 375°F, and bake until the juices are bubbling and the crumble topping has turned a rich pecan-colored brown, another 30 to 45 minutes. Allow the pie to set, at room temperature, for at least 2 hours or—better yet, overnight— before serving.

BEVERAGES

PHOENICIA DINER BLOODY MARY

Makes 2 cups slurry, enough for 10 drinks

A lot of diners don't serve alcohol. Their reasons are valid—liquor licenses are expensive and difficult to get, and stocking a bar is a big investment. For a diner whose customers tend to drop in for a bite and then hurry out the door, avoiding the nuisance of it all makes good sense. But when we reopened the Phoenicia Diner, we wanted to encourage people to slow their rolls, to linger a while over a drink and conversation. We are, after all, on the edge of the Catskills, where people come to get away from it all for a night, for a weekend, for the rest of their lives. Use this recipe to replicate that moment of pause and respite at home.

Bloody Marys are often blended in a big pitcher (you can conjure the image, long celery stick and all), but we do it a bit differently here, making the spicy slurry in advance and keeping it separate from the tomato juice and alcohol until you're ready for a drink. The nice thing about this recipe is that it works equally well for single servings (make your slurry, then use it, as needed, over the course of a couple of weeks) or for a batch of cocktails for a gathering.

1. **Make the slurry:** Place all the slurry ingredients in a pitcher or large jar and stir vigorously to combine. (Slurry will keep for up to 2 weeks sealed in the refrigerator. Just give the mixture a good stir before using.)

2. **Make the drinks:** For each serving, fill a tall glass with plenty of ice and add the vodka and 3 tablespoons slurry. Add the tomato juice and stir to combine. Garnish with your favorite items.

FOR THE SLURRY

½ cup **fresh lemon juice** (from 2 to 3 large, juicy lemons)

½ cup **prepared hot horseradish**, drained (we use Gold's)

⅓ cup preferred **hot sauce** (we use Valentina)

¾ cup **Worcestershire sauce**

1 teaspoon **celery salt**

½ teaspoon freshly ground **black pepper**

FOR EACH DRINK

1½ ounces (3 tablespoons) **premium vodka**

4 ounces (½ cup) best-quality **tomato juice** (we use Migliorelli)

Assorted garnish items (such as celery stalks, pickled okra, jícama slices, and stuffed olives)

Bootleggers of the Catskills

Dutch and Legs are two of the most notorious bootleggers in our nation's history—men who got fat when America went dry. And it was here, in the Catskills, that they found a particularly suitable haven for their crooked ways.

In 1920, when Prohibition became the law of the land, the number of drinking establishments in New York shot up. The necessity of keeping operations covert only upped the ante and sweetened the brew for nefarious characters looking to make a buck. The Catskills quickly revealed itself to be an ideal cog in the bootlegging machine that kept New Yorkers buzzed throughout the roaring twenties: remote enough to offer protection, but close enough to the thrumming center of New York to reap the fruits of the city's economic power.

Dutch Schultz, né Arthur Flegenheimer, was a Bronx-born German Jew. He learned at the elbow of Arnold Rothstein, the "Moses of the Mafia," and as Prohibition took hold, he accrued a number of stills in the Catskills and a home just outside the village of Phoenicia. Dutch kept a hold on his market by bumping off his competitors—down in the city those hits were carefully orchestrated, while Upstate the approach was a bit more Wild West: shootouts and drownings in isolated mountain lakes, with a local code of silence shielding Dutch and his operations. In 1933, when the liquor laws were loosened, Dutch found his way into other operations: numbers games, Tammany Hall, and the unions. He and several of his associates joined forces with the Sicilian mob, creating a powerful ring of organized crime that struck fear into New Yorkers for years. Dutch was gunned down in Newark in 1935, at the age of thirty-three, but not before being named Public Enemy Number One by J. Edgar Hoover, and after allegedly burying a fortune of between five and seven million dollars in cash somewhere in Phoenicia. Though Dutch left a hand-drawn treasure map, no one has ever been able to locate the bounty, though the hunt still occasionally draws fortune-seeking dreamers.

What Dutch wrought from the small Ulster County town of Phoenicia, Jack "Legs" Diamond effected in Greene County. From the village of Acra, he shepherded booze down from Canada and controlled an enormous share of the brewing and distilling activity in the region, employing a massive ring of brewers, distillers, drivers, guards, and even sheriffs. Legs was resourceful, making use of the area's existing resources: The Kingston brewery formerly known as Barmann was ground zero for his beer operation, which snaked through the city's sewer system to a nearby warehouse before barrels were loaded into trucks bound for Manhattan and Albany. Many of the tunnels that aided the operation were discovered in the 1970s, including one in the pine-shaded backyard of a Kingston rectory. And the region's ample apple orchards provided Legs with the cider he needed to distill potent applejack, literally a "jacked up" (read: boozier) version of hard cider.

While the erstwhile characters of Prohibition are long gone, a taste for the strong stuff never died. Ralph Erenzo, founder of Ulster County's Tuthilltown Spirits, helped spur the Farm Distillery Act in New York State, which has catalyzed a major resurgence in distilling in the Hudson Valley and Catskills. In 2007, Governor Eliot Spitzer signed the act, establishing licensing for small, agriculturally based distillers to produce, hold tastings for, and sell up to 35,000 gallons a year—the first major legislative rollback of Prohibition-era regulations in the state. What began as an effort led by three policy-pushing Hudson Valley farm distilleries has grown into a bona fide movement, with nearly 150 small- and medium-scale distilleries operating statewide at the time of this writing.

The changes in New York's policy have given a leg up to the craft distilling world, but have also boosted related industries, including malting and barrel making. These days, it's common to see New York State spirits lining the top shelves of bars in the city and country alike. And while urban distilleries have popped up in competition with their rural predecessors, areas like the Catskills continue to provide the vast majority of raw agricultural materials being used in micro-distilleries; farm-to-bottle is now as buzzy a moniker as farm-to-table. Since the Diner's opening, we've been fortunate to be able to add a number of ultra-local products to our bar, including vodka from Union Grove Distillery (which we use in our Bloody Mary, page 247), and beer from West Kill Brewery, Keegan Ales, and Woodstock Brewery, the last a mere stone's throw from us on Route 28.

While today there's no need to seek out a speakeasy to enjoy a locally sourced drink, recalling the outlaws of yore adds a little thrill to our glasses in the here and now.

AGUAS FRESCAS

Serves 1

FOR EACH SERVING

¾ cup **fresh fruit juice**

1½ teaspoons **fresh lemon juice**

1½ teaspoons **simple syrup** (see Note)

2 tablespoons **seltzer water**

Aguas frescas, simply a combination of fresh fruit juice and a bit of water, are one of the many ingenious culinary inventions we can thank Mexico for. At the Diner, we make several versions in summer, when refreshing beverages are in high demand, using seltzer water for a little extra pizzazz.

Use the best-quality fruit you can find. With a fresh, perfectly ripe watermelon, pineapple, or cucumber, you won't need much, if any, sweetener. The proportions here are a starting point—taste your fruit juice before fiddling with it, and add more simple syrup and fresh lemon juice as you like to achieve a refreshingly tart, but still sweet, balance.

For the fresh fruit juice: To juice your fruit, use a home juicer on the lowest setting, or puree the fruit in a blender and strain it through a fine-mesh sieve.

WATERMELON: The watermelons you find at a farmers market in high season tend to be smaller, fully ripe, and far sweeter than those at other times. When watermelons are at their peak, they don't need any extra sweetening, so we omit the simple syrup altogether. If you're buying watermelons in a supermarket, assume they were picked a little shy of ripe and will be less juicy than a vine-ripened melon. You'll need 3 to 4 cups of cubed commercial watermelon for 1 serving (6 ounces) of juice, a little less with a farmers market melon.

PINEAPPLE: 1 ripe whole pineapple will yield about 1½ cups, or 12 ounces, of juice, which is enough for 2 servings.

CUCUMBER-MINT: 1 large seedless (English hothouse) cucumber, juiced together with 2 fresh mint leaves, yields 12 ounces, or 1½ cups, of juice. Reserve a sprig of fresh mint leaves for each serving.

To prepare the beverage: Fill a 16-ounce glass three-fourths full with ice cubes. Stir in the fruit juice, then taste for sweetness and tartness, adding lemon juice and simple syrup to your liking. Top with seltzer, give a stir, and enjoy.

NOTE: Simple syrup is merely a 1:1 ratio of sugar to water that has been heated and stirred just until the sugar dissolves, then removed from the heat and cooled. One cup of sugar and 1 cup of water yields about 1½ cups simple syrup.

4 **lemons**

½ cup **sugar**

3 cups **cold water**,
plus more as needed

CLASSIC LEMONADE

Serves 4

Nothing beats a tall glass of chilled lemonade on a hot summer day. Unlike many lemonade recipes, this one makes use of the entire lemon. Here, we unlock lemons' flavorful essential oils by boiling the zest, along with sugar and water, to make an infused simple syrup. Combined with the lemons' fresh juice, this is an extra-refreshing, decidedly lemony version of the classic summer drink.

1. Using a citrus zester or vegetable peeler, remove the zest in strips from the lemons.

2. Place the sugar, lemon zest, and ½ cup water in a small saucepan and bring to a boil over high heat. Once the simple syrup boils, remove it from the heat and allow it to cool.

3. While the mixture is cooling, juice all 4 lemons into a pitcher and remove the seeds.

4. Strain the syrup through a fine-mesh sieve into the lemon juice and stir to blend. Add the water, then taste, adding more water as you like. Serve in tall glasses filled with ice cubes.

GROWN-UP HOT CHOCOLATE

Serves 4

Whether our guests come in rosy-cheeked and clad in swishy snow pants after a day on the slopes or stomping their boots after digging their car out of a snowbank, we're constantly reminded of how long winter is here in the Catskills. Hot chocolate is one of our soul-warmers, an extra boost for the snow-happy and a balm for winter's doldrums.

This is grown-up hot chocolate (though we've seen plenty of kids have their way with it); it's a bit bitter and even floral from really good dark chocolate (we use Fruition), and with a hint of saltiness to offset the sweetness. We serve this without adornment--it's rich enough as is—but you could certainly add whipped cream if you feel like taking the decadence to the next level.

3 cups **whole milk**

1 cup **half-and-half**

¼ cup **sugar**

¼ teaspoon **kosher salt**

4 ounces 65–70% high-quality **dark chocolate**, finely chopped

1 teaspoon **vanilla extract**

1. In a medium saucepan, combine the milk, half-and-half, sugar, and salt. Over medium-high heat, heat the mixture until it just begins to bubble around the edges.

2. Turn the heat down to medium-low and add the chopped chocolate, whisking until fully melted and incorporated. Stir in the vanilla. Divide among 4 mugs and serve.

PHOENICIA DINER MILKSHAKE

Serves 1

Milkshakes: delicious, nostalgic, and indulgent enough to make anyone feel like a kid again. At the Diner, we keep it classic: vanilla, chocolate, and strawberry. But by all means, use whichever flavor of ice cream you like best. If you're gonna have a milkshake, it should be exactly the way you want it! For some, that means mixing grown-up and childhood pleasures; to make this milkshake boozy, reduce the milk by half and add a shot of bourbon.

Simple syrup may seem like a superfluous addition here, but it helps the milkshake retain the ice cream's sweetness after the addition of the milk. Feel free to omit it, though, if you prefer your milkshakes less sweet.

This recipe batches well. Multiply the proportions here to make as many milkshakes as your blender will accommodate. Just be sure to leave a few inches of headspace. A shot glass is a helpful measuring tool here.

3 scoops **favorite ice cream** (¾ cup, or about 6 ounces; we use Ronnybrook), frozen very hard

2 tablespoons **simple syrup** (see Note, page 250)

¼ cup **whole milk** (or 2 tablespoons milk and 2 tablespoons bourbon)

1. Combine the ice cream, simple syrup, and milk in a blender and whizz until a light, frothy head has developed on top and the mixture is very smooth.

2. Serve the milkshake immediately in a tall chilled glass.

HOT MULLED APPLE CIDER

Makes 1 gallon

1 gallon **unfiltered apple cider**

3 **cinnamon sticks**

5 **whole allspice berries**

12 **whole cloves**

7 **star anise**

Pinch of grated **nutmeg**

2-inch piece of **fresh ginger**, peeled and sliced ¼ inch thick

1 **orange**, cut into ⅛-inch rounds

1 **lemon**, cut into ⅛-inch rounds

The common orchard apple—*Malus pumila*, if you want to get all scientific about it—has been abundant in the middle and upper Hudson Valley region since the European settlers began planting orchards here in the 1600s to replace the native crabapples. For nearly as long, it's been an important cash crop for the region, as well as a seasonal tourist draw. What to do with all that fruit? Anything and everything: the apples show up all over in New York State cuisine—sweet and savory, food and drink. Pure apple cider—unsweetened, unfiltered, and if you can manage to find it from a noncommercial press, unpasteurized—is a favorite around here. On a chilly fall afternoon after a hike in peak foliage or on a snowy winter day on the slopes, a hot mug of this stuff, mulled with warming spices and a bit of citrus, just can't be beat.

1. Place all the ingredients in a heavy-bottomed stockpot or Dutch oven. Bring to a boil over high heat, then cover and reduce to the lowest heat possible.

2. Let the flavors infuse for at least 1 hour (the longer the better), and then ladle into your favorite mugs. (Alternatively, place all the ingredients in a slow cooker, set on high heat, then lower the heat and mull for at least 1 hour.)

CHOCOLATE EGG CREAM

Serves 1

Egg creams are a soda-fountain classic and used to be mainstays in drugstores in New York City. Sadly, they've lost their popularity. We aim to bring them back. There's something oddly addictive about the combination of creamy milk, nose-tickling seltzer water, and chocolate syrup.

Opinions run strong when it comes to egg creams, as they do with most foods and drinks that stir nostalgia. While we can't police your kitchen, we strongly recommend you use Fox's U-Bet chocolate syrup, the classic foundation for this classic drink. Also, we give a range for the amount of seltzer here, which is meant to accommodate variations in the size of the soda glass you're using. You want the egg cream—once it's assembled and stirred and the head has formed—to completely fill the glass.

½ cup ice-cold **whole milk**

¾ to 1 cup chilled **seltzer water**

3 tablespoons **Fox's U-Bet chocolate syrup**

1. Put the milk into a chilled tall soda glass. Pour the seltzer into the glass in a thin stream from at least 6 to 8 inches above the rim, filling the glass until it is about 1 inch from the top. Use a long teaspoon to vigorously stir the bottom of the liquid to create a thick, foamy white head.

2. Gently pour the chocolate syrup down the inside edge of the glass. Use the long teaspoon to again stir the liquid vigorously at the bottom, making sure not to disturb the head (stirring for too long will destroy the foam). Drink immediately.

ACKNOWLEDGMENTS

From Mike: My life is full of examples of "good things come to those who wait" or, more accurately, "those not looking for it," and when I got an email out of the blue from our editor Jenn Sit it proved true once again. Thank you, Jenn, for seeing the potential in our little restaurant before we did. Big thanks to Sara and Chris for the hard work you put into the birth of this book, along with Johnny and Charlotte for some of the best photos and laughs of any cookbook project ever. Thank you to the rest of our stellar team at Clarkson Potter, including Ian Dingman, Stephanie Huntwork, Mark McCauslin, and Heather Williamson.

The Phoenicia Diner success story is not based on a single person; it's been built on the backs of the people who worked to get it off the ground, local guests who supported us during the early years, and those who took the job and leap of faith of working here when its future was seriously clouded in mystery.

Credit should go to the concept builders including our social media guru Holley Atkinson, our gifted branding/logo creator Gabriele Wilson, and our consultant Olivia Tincani and Jason Wood for our amazing opening menu. My deep gratitude goes to the local restaurant owners, Marybeth and Devin of the Peekamoose Restaurant, Michael Koegel of Mamasboy Burgers, and Jack Zamor of the Arkville Bread and Breakfast, who took the time to pass along their wisdom about restaurant life.

To the longtime FOH staff who took a chance on me and are still helping me learn the business: Charlene, Mona, Lisa, Nicole, Amber, and Thomasina. The rock-solid BOH who grind it out no matter the difficulty, heat, or outlandish food request: Humberto, our egg machine, who must hold an unofficial record for perfectly cooking sunny-side up eggs thousands of times over a busy weekend, and Jésus, who can magically do the work of three people in the kitchen as well as fix the plumbing and repair equipment, all the while with a smile on his face. A special thank-you to Mel, our first chef and kitchen manager, who helped figure out how to go from 150 covers a day to 5 times that on a busy summer weekend. These people are the soul and backbone on which the Phoenicia Diner built

its reputation and deserve more credit than they ever receive. I can't manage a day without guidance from Christine Gonzalez, who has the catchall phrased job of Project Manager, which means everything that falls through the cracks. And finally a special thanks to our General Manager Courtney Malsatzki for her deep sense of style and caring, which come through in everything she does, and her uncanny ability to remain calm and collected when all seems like chaos to me. Courtney and her staff, especially her assistant, Daisy, make the Diner hum along like a well-oiled 1962 chrome-plated machine.

And to the local folks in Phoenicia, New York, who welcomed and supported us when we opened through some rough service days when we would run out of bacon or coffee because we simply could not keep up, or who volunteered to help move some equipment or dig a foundation. There are so many of you, including Dolly, Pam and Eddie, Honey, and George the local police officer who also is more of a foodie than even I am. Kenny along with his wife, Naomi, are my de facto godparents on all things local and mountain-based. Kenny even found me once on the side of the road after my motorcycle and I missed a curve. I was still dazed and confused as he drove up with his dump truck and called an ambulance, even followed it to the hospital to take me home after some patchwork to my leg. David and June, who were some of our first customers, would constantly encourage me to not take any criticism personally. David, especially, since he was kindred soul who was a chef back in NYC and knew all I was going through in the early days and would calmly joke about how insignificant some customer complaint about burnt toast was in the grand scheme of things. David has since passed, but I still conjure him up in difficult moments to make me laugh. There is Donna and Harold, who came in a few times each week to support us. Harold, sadly, has also passed on, but Donna still arrives each week to order any veggie dish of the day and catch up on the news with me.

Finally, to my family: My love for our two daughters, Ryan and Logan, is bottomless. These two spent months prior to our opening listening to me obsess over color samples and branding ideas and, after opening and twelve-hour days, "volunteering" to work at the Diner on weekends bussing, running, and cashiering when they both had more pressing things to do (like schoolwork or hanging out with friends). What can I say to my wife and childhood sweetheart who threw her support behind an outlandish project, not because it was a good idea (it wasn't at the time) or had a solid business plan (I had none), but solely because it was something that would reinvigorate my spirit. That is the kind of selfless act that can only be repaid with undying love and gratitude. I have an endless supply of each for her.

From Chris: My culinary skills and stylistic leanings have been influenced by every single hustling cook, rock-star dishwasher, big-named chef, and big-dreaming sous I have ever worked alongside, and I owe you all a warm plate of gratitude garnished with much respect. A grand thank-you goes to the whole Phoenicia Diner crew, especially Humberto and Jésus, for picking up my slack while I figured out how to scale down recipes built to feed a large army of urbanites famished from tramping through the woods and swimming in the holes. Much appreciation is also due to Mike and Helene for reviving the Diner and giving me the chance to make my mark on what will surely be a long and successful run. Calvin and Eliza, you have managed a miracle by somehow shrinking my life until it feels like little more than baby–work–sleep, while at the same time expanding my world infinitely with just a laugh or the simple word "More?" I will always be grateful that you helped me trim away the excesses and find true abundance. And Sara, you are a true superwoman. How can a normal mortal find the time to write a cookbook while publishing and touring for another book and teaching university classes and feeding, cleaning, wrangling, and loving the twins and keeping me on task and tending to our garden and stocking our pantry and freezer and, and, and. . . . I will always be in your debt, and I'm glad you've given me a lifetime to pay it back.

From Sara: Cookbooks are *much* bigger projects than they appear from the outside. My sincere thanks to the small army of recipe testers—especially the immaculate Jenn Anderson—whose ability to meet deadlines and finicky-ness kept us on point. Thanks to Mike Cioffi and Helene Banks for giving Chris the opportunity that began the Upstate chapter of our life. To Jenn Sit—I liked you immediately, and I've liked you more with each subsequent interaction: you're a straight shooter, a calm presence, and a true professional. It's a pleasure to write for your keen eye. To the entire team at Potter, thank you for your vision and your hard work; it's a real privilege to be an author on your list. To Johnny and Charlotte Autry, we were lucky to get in while your stars were rising, and I have no doubt that soon you'll outshine us all. To the friends, family, neighbors, caregivers, and babysitters (especially Danila Monteiro, nanny-cum-*tia* extraordinaire) who helped me get back to work after Cal and Eliza were born, and bolstered me as I figured out how to become a working mom, know that there would be no bylines without you; my gratitude knows no bounds. Speaking of Cal and Eliza, I'm sorry your dad and I weren't home more during that summer of 2018, when this project ramped up and work stole too much of our attention. That summer taught us a lot about life, work, and family, and helped us figure out how we wanted to raise you both. Know that life's most important lessons rarely come easy. And finally, thanks to Chris, with whom I'm on this crazy journey every day: my modern lover, the donkey to my zebra. Your hoodie and cooking may have first caught my attention, but you've kept my heart.

INDEX

Published in the United States by Clarkson Potter/Publishers, an imprint of Random House, a division of Penguin Random House LLC, New York.
clarksonpotter.com

Library of Congress Cataloging-in-Publication Data
Names: Cioffi, Mike, author. | Bradley, Chris (Chef), author. | Franklin, Sara B., author. | Autry, Johnny, photograher.
Title: The Phoenicia Diner Cookbook: Dishes and Dispatches from the Catskill Mountains / Mike Cioffi, Chris Bradley, and Sara B. Franklin; photographs by Johnny Autry.
Description: First edition. | New York: Clarkson Potter/Publishers, 2020. | Includes index.
Identifiers: LCCN 2019029598 (print) | LCCN 2019029599 (ebook) | ISBN 9780525575139 (hardcover) | ISBN 9780525575146 (ebook)
Subjects: LCSH: Cooking, American. | Phoenicia Diner (Phoenicia, NY) | LCGFT: Cookbooks.
Classification: LCC TX715 .C569 2020 (print) | LCC TX715 (ebook) | DDC 641.5973–dc23
LC record available at https://lccn.loc.gov/2019029598.
LC ebook record available at https://lccn.loc.gov/2019029599.

ISBN 978-0-525-57513-9
Ebook ISBN 978-0-525-57514-6

Printed in China

Book and cover design by Ian Dingman
Photographs by Johnny Autry
Illustrations by Joel Holland and Gabriele Wilson Design

10 9 8 7 6 5 4 3 2 1

First Edition

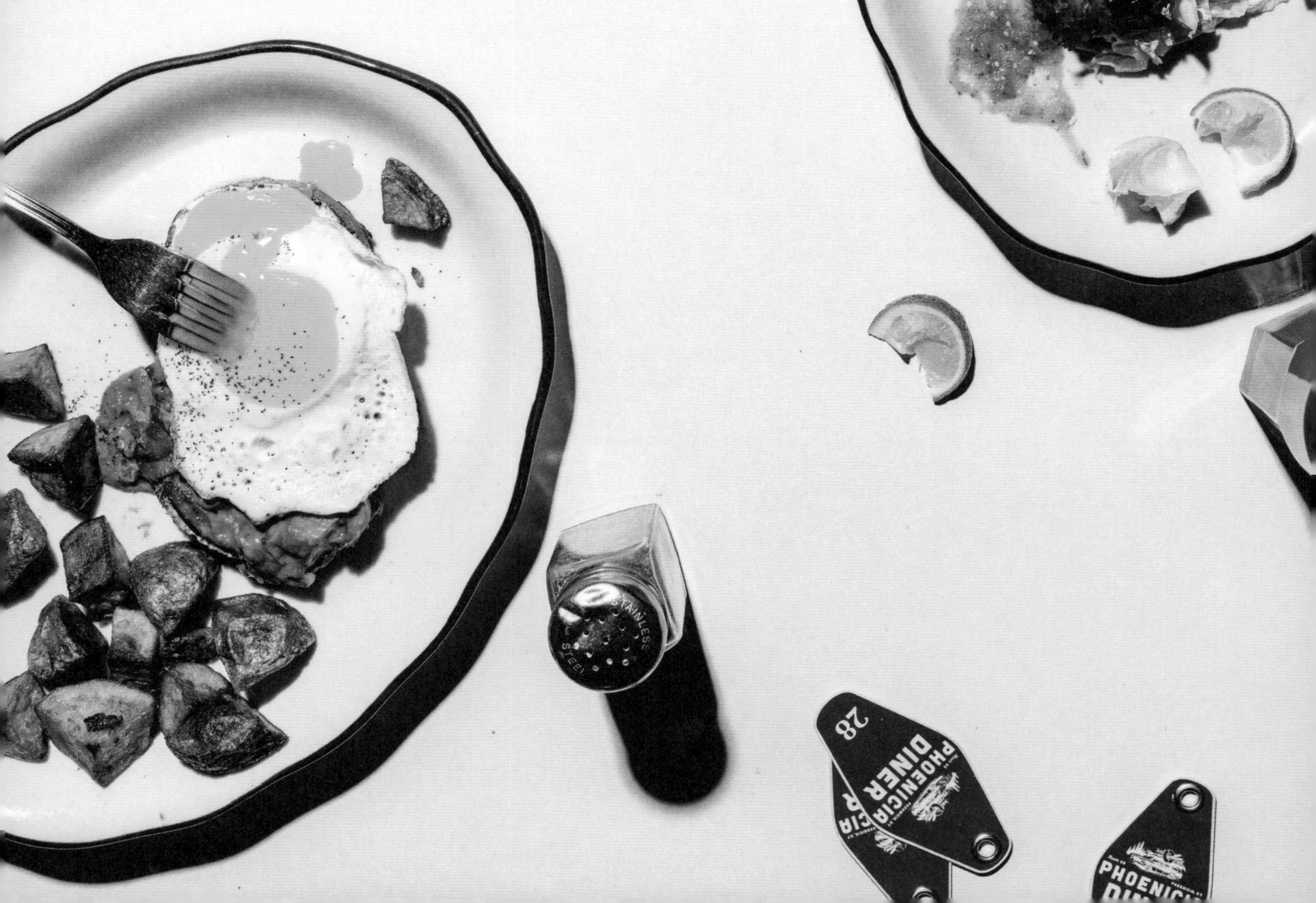

MIKE CIOFFI is the creator and visionary behind the Phoenicia Diner. After a thirty-year career building scenery for television and Broadway shows, he became interested in the restaurant world, and in 2012 he and his family took a leap of faith when the revamped Diner opened its doors.

CHEF CHRIS BRADLEY spent two decades cooking in some of the most renowned restaurants in New York and Washington, DC, including Gramercy Tavern and Untitled at the Whitney, before moving to Upstate New York. He now lives with his family in the Hudson Valley.

SARA B. FRANKLIN is a writer and a professor of food culture and history at NYU's Gallatin School for Individualized Study and the NYU Prison Education Program. She lives with her family in the Hudson Valley.

CLARKSON POTTER/PUBLISHERS
NEW YORK
clarksonpotter.com

Also available as an ebook

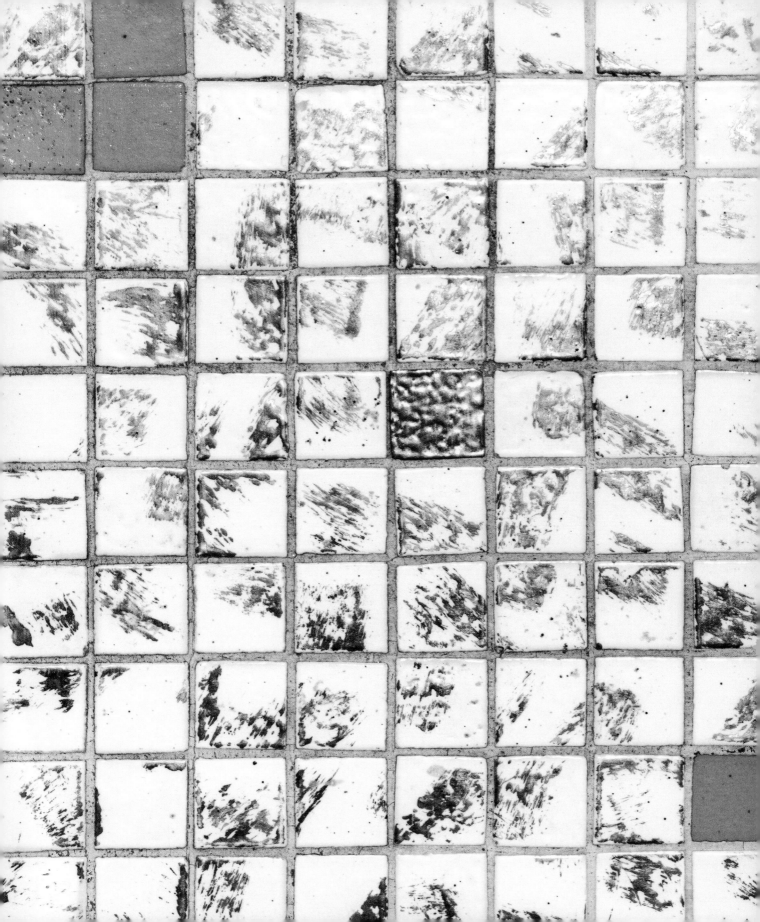